GREAT COMMUNICATOR:
The Story of Ronald Reagan

GREAT COMMUNICATOR:
The Story of Ronald Reagan

Jeff C. Young

**MORGAN
REYNOLDS**
Publishing, Inc.

620 South Elm Street, Suite 223
Greensboro, North Carolina 27406
http://www.morganreynolds.com

GREAT COMMUNICATOR: THE STORY OF RONALD REAGAN

Library of Congress Cataloging-in-Publication Data

Young, Jeff C., 1948-
  Great communicator : the story of Ronald Reagan / Jeff C. Young.— 1st
ed.
    v. cm. — (Twentieth century leaders)
Includes bibliographical references and index.
Contents: "Drama, Politics and Sports" — Sportscaster to movie star —
Transitions — Un-American activities — Politics and television —
Governor Reagan — Campaigning for president — Second try — President
Reagan — Morning in America — Perestroika — Last years.
  ISBN 1-931798-10-9 (lib. bdg.)
  1. Reagan, Ronald—Juvenile literature. 2. Presidents—United
States—Biography—Juvenile literature. [1. Reagan, Ronald. 2.
Presidents.] I. Title. II. Series.
  E877.Y68 2003
  973.927'092—dc21

                          2002155919

Printed in the United States of America
First Edition

Notable Americans

Ronald Reagan

Dolley Madison

Thomas Jefferson

John Adams

Andrew Jackson

Alexander Hamilton

George W. Bush

Lyndon Baines Johnson

Dwight D. Eisenhower

Ishi

Richard Nixon

Madeleine Albright

Lou Henry Hoover

Thurgood Marshall

Petticoat Spies

William Tecumseh Sherman

Mary Todd Lincoln

To my nephew, Michael David Hundley.

Contents

Ronald Reagan, 1984.
(*Courtesy of the Ronald Reagan Library.*)

Chapter One

"Drama, Politics and Sports"

Ronald Reagan once said he became president because of an unsuccessful job interview. "If I'd gotten the job I wanted at Montgomery Ward, I suppose I would have never left Illinois," he said.

The failed interview happened in the summer of 1932, at the height of the Great Depression. Twenty-one-year-old Reagan was a recent college graduate with a degree in economics and a soon-to-end summer job as a lifeguard. He did not need a degree in economics to know jobs were scarce that year. The unemployment rate was over twenty-six percent.

Earlier in the summer, Ronald left his home in Dixon, Illinois, and hitchhiked to Chicago to look for work as a radio announcer. He had a clear, pleasant voice and plenty of public speaking experience from participating in college debates and acting in plays. He soon discovered that was not enough. Chicago was too big a market to crack for a young man without radio experience. "All

I got was rejection," Reagan recalled. "No one wanted an inexperienced kid, especially during the Depression."

After returning to Dixon, downcast and dispirited, Ronald got some encouraging news from his father. The Montgomery Ward Company was opening a store in town and was looking for a sporting goods manager. In the interview, Reagan told the store manager he would run the best sporting goods department Montgomery Ward had ever seen. The manager may have mistook confidence for cockiness; Reagan did not get the job. He resumed looking for work in radio and a short time later was hired as a weekend sportscaster for station WOC in Davenport, Iowa.

This job was the break of a lifetime. Broadcasting led to acting, acting led to politics, and politics led to the White House as America's fortieth president.

Ronald Wilson Reagan was born in Tampico, Illinois, on February 6, 1911. With a population of only 849 people, Tampico did not have a doctor, so Ronald's mother went through labor in the family's apartment above the general store Ronald's father managed. The midwife informed Ronald's mother her baby was breach and would be born feet forward. This was a dangerous situation. Fortunately, a physician who had been stranded in Tampico by a snowstorm the day before was able to come over and deliver the ten-pound baby. It was Ronald's large size that reminded his father of a fat and prosperous Dutchman, and the nickname Dutch stuck from birth.

His father, John Edward Reagan, was a handsome,

An early Reagan family photo. Ronald Reagan is at the bottom right, beside his brother, Neil. Father Jack worked as a salesman and store manager, while mother Nelle devoted herself to raising her sons. (*Courtesy of the Ronald Reagan Library.*)

athletic man most people knew as Jack. He worked in retail sales as a shoe salesman and store clerk. He was a good-hearted and intelligent man who struggled his entire life with an alcohol problem. He was not abusive to his family, but there were frequent job and address changes. Between the ages of six and ten, Ronald attended a different school every year.

Reagan's mother, Nelle Wilson, met Jack while shopping. They were married in 1904. Their first son, John Neil, was born in 1909. Jack was Catholic and insisted that Neil be baptized in the same faith. Nelle was an active member of the Disciples of Christ church. When

Ronald was born two years later, she decided to raise him in her denomination. Nelle Reagan was a warm-hearted and compassionate woman who regularly visited sick neighbors. Her compassion extended to her husband's alcoholism. She told her two sons that Jack suffered from a sickness, and they should never condemn their father for something he could not control.

In spite of his father's drinking, his family's constant moving, and lack of material things, Reagan always maintained his childhood was the happiest time of his life. He credits his parents with teaching him to follow his dreams. "I learned from my father the value of hard work and ambition. From my mother I learned the value of prayer, how to have dreams and believe I could make them come true."

When Reagan was ten, his family moved to Dixon, Illinois—a town of less than nine thousand residents. The family moved five times within the city limits, but the town of Dixon would remain Ronald's home until he was twenty-one. His brother, Neil, remembered that although Ronald had friends wherever they lived, he did not seek others out and often kept to himself.

A year after moving to Dixon, Reagan heard his first radio broadcast. One of the neighbors had an early crystal set, which received a signal by connecting a wire to a crystal. On a wintry day, Ronald, Neil, and a group of children carried the radio around town, trying to pick up a signal. Suddenly, having moved under a bridge, the boys heard a brief snatch of music and then an announcer's voice coming over the air. This was a significant moment in Ronald's life. He was listening to a transmission from out of the sky—rather than over telegraph or phone wire.

Reagan entered high school at the age of thirteen. In his first autobiography, *Where's the Rest of Me?*, he wrote, "I loved three things: drama, politics and sports." He played basketball and football and ran track. He served as the president of the student body during his senior year and acted in school plays.

Summers he worked. From 1926 to 1933, Reagan had a job as a lifeguard at a local park. He presided over a sandy beach on the Rock River. Over those seven years, he later said, he saved seventy-seven people from drowning, and few of them ever thanked him.

Neither of Reagan's parents had even been able to go to high school, but Ronald received an athletic scholarship to cover half of his tuition at Eureka College in Eureka, Illinois. Money saved from his lifeguard job helped to pay his bills. He also got free meals for waiting on tables and washing dishes at the Tau Kappa Epsilon fraternity house and a local diner. Coaching the college's swimming team also provided him an income.

In the fall of 1928, Reagan got his first taste of politics when he became a student activist. The stock market crash was still about a year away, but the farming areas felt the economic slowdown sooner than Wall Street, and Eureka College was having severe financial problems. School administrators worried the college would have to be closed down. The administration decided to lay off some of the faculty and eliminate courses.

The cutbacks were scheduled to be implemented over the Thanksgiving break.

When students and faculty learned of the plan, they were outraged. The budget cuts would cancel classes many needed for graduation. A student committee was formed to discuss a student strike. Reagan was chosen as the freshman class representative.

The committee presented a petition to the school's board of trustees, calling for the resignation of the college's president, Bert Wilson. The trustees refused its demands and the student committee held a midnight meeting just before Thanksgiving. When Reagan's turn came to speak, he jumped up and made an emotional pitch in favor of a student strike. "Giving that speech— my first—was as exciting as any I ever gave. For the first time in my life, I felt my words reach out and grab an audience, after a while it was as if the audience and I were one."

Reagan's impassioned and rousing speech had the desired effect. The student body voted to go on strike and unanimously adopted a written statement asking for the school president's resignation. They proceeded to boycott classes while cooperative professors ignored their absences. The students kept up with their required work. After one week, the school president resigned, the proposed layoffs were canceled, and Ronald Reagan realized he had a special gift for public speaking.

Like countless other college students, Reagan experimented with alcohol. As the child of an alcoholic father, he was aware of its destructive potential, but he

While a teenager, Ronald Reagan worked as a lifeguard for seven summers at a beach on the Rock River, where he saved seventy-seven people from drowning. (*Courtesy of the Ronald Reagan Library.*)

was still curious enough to acquire some firsthand experience. At that time, the country was under Prohibition, which made the possession of alcoholic beverages illegal. Reagan and his fraternity friends found a way around that. Two of them worked for a physician and had free use of his apartment. One evening, they acquired some bootleg liquor. Inexperienced at drinking, Reagan overdid it. "When the bottle came to me, I'd take a big drink, as if it was a bottle of soda pop." In a short time he was roaring drunk. His friends smuggled him into the fraternity house and put him in the shower to sober him up. Reagan wrote that was the last and only time he got drunk. "I'd been taught a lesson. I decided if that's what you get for drinking—a sense of helplessness—I didn't want any part of it."

The feeling of wanting to be in control led Reagan to acting and public speaking. He was also influenced by his theatrical parents who acted in local plays. Reagan's good looks and unassuming manner won him the lead role in most of the school productions. The plays were performed without microphones, but Reagan had no trouble projecting his voice to the last row of seats. He also honed his speaking skills as a member of the college's debate team.

Although he was fond of the theater, Reagan was even fonder of sports. Football was his favorite. His teammates remembered him as a player of modest talent, but great enthusiasm. His college coach, Ralph McKinzie, recalled Reagan had a great knowledge of the game, but average ability. "[He] just couldn't execute what he knew on the playing field. But he never gave up trying."

Reagan had more success in swimming and track, and won a varsity letter in both sports. He also took part in many extracurricular activities. Reagan was a cheerleader for the basketball team, president of the student council and booster club, feature editor of the school yearbook, and a reporter for the school newspaper. Although he was a natural leader and well liked, he had many acquaintances but no close friends.

Sports, along with his other activities, left him little time for studying. Reagan was a C student, and Eureka was not known as an academically demanding college. Thanks to a near photographic memory and an ability to quickly memorize facts, he did not have to study hard to pass his classes. In his two autobiographies, which are full of college memories, Reagan never mentions academics.

Reagan's brother, Neil, also graduated from Eureka College. Neil recalled a professor once complained that Reagan never opened a book. Still, when it was test time, he knew enough to pass the course. According to Neil, Reagan would wait until the night before a test, open the textbook, "and in about a quick hour he would thumb through it and photograph those pages and write a good test."

Winning an acting award while attending college meant more to Reagan than academic honors. In his junior year, Eureka College was one of the twelve schools invited to participate in a prestigious theatrical competition at Northwestern University.

The students from Eureka performed a one-act play by Edna St. Vincent Millay entitled "Aria da Capo." Set in ancient Greece, the play had an anti-war theme. Reagan played a shepherd who is strangled to death. Eureka placed second in the competition, and Reagan was one of three students to receive an individual acting award. After the competition, the head of Northwestern's Speech Department told Reagan he should think about making acting his career. He was flattered but felt it was an impractical goal. Yet, he did not completely dismiss the idea. "By my senior year at

Eureka, my secret dream to be an actor was firmly planted, but I knew that in the middle of Illinois in 1932, I couldn't go around saying, I want to be an actor."

Reagan came up with an alternative plan. Radio was another form of show business, and he had a pleasant baritone voice and plenty of speaking experience. Sports broadcasting on the radio sounded to him like the ideal job. Getting paid to watch a football or baseball game would be a great way to make a living.

In June 1932, Reagan graduated from Eureka College with a bachelor's degree in economics and sociology. America was in the midst of a terrible economic depression, and with one in four Americans out of work, Reagan had no job offers. Due to the Depression, his father, Jack, had lost his investment in a shoe store. It was an election year, and Reagan's father threw himself into the campaign for Democratic presidential candidate Franklin D. Roosevelt. Jack was Catholic and a Democrat, which was unusual in the predominantly Protestant and Republican Midwest. His campaigning paid off. After Roosevelt's election, he was appointed to run the local welfare office. Ronald supported Roosevelt's campaign as well, and the Depression-era president was his first political hero.

Reagan returned to Dixon for another summer of lifeguarding. By August, he still had no job offers. After being rejected by the big stations in Chicago, and being refused the job at Montgomery Ward, Reagan started calling on some of the smaller stations around Dixon.

Franklin D. Roosevelt and Herbert Hoover on the way to Roosevelt's inauguration in 1933. *(Courtesy of the Library of Congress.)*

He got his first break at station WOC in Davenport, Iowa. The station manager, Peter MacArthur, initially turned Reagan away. He told him they had just hired an announcer after auditioning ninety-five candidates. Reagan, frustrated and angry, blurted out, "How in the hell does a guy ever get to be a sports announcer if he can't get inside a station?"

Reagan began walking away. MacArthur stopped him before he got on the elevator. He asked Reagan if he knew anything about football. Reagan told him he had played the game for eight years in high school and college. Then MacArthur asked, "Could you tell me about a football game and make me see it as if I was home listening to the radio?" Reagan told him he was sure he could.

MacArthur led Reagan into a studio and sat him in front of a microphone. He told Reagan to start talking when the red light came on and he would be listening. Reagan was finally getting the opportunity he yearned for. His mind raced as he tried to think up imaginary players and plays. Fortunately, Reagan had an exceptional memory and a lively imagination. He put both of them to use.

Reagan remembered a football game he had played at Eureka. It was a game his team had won in the final twenty seconds on a sixty-five-yard run by the quarterback. When the red light flashed on, Reagan began talking, "Here we are in the fourth quarter with Western State University leading Eureka six to nothing . . ."

For about twenty minutes, Reagan improvised. He described both teams running up and down the field before Eureka's big play tied the game. Then he described the point after touchdown that gave them a seven-to-six win. He concluded by saying, "We return you now to our main studio."

MacArthur was delighted by his performance. He told Reagan to come back to the studio the following Saturday to broadcast the Iowa-Bradley University game. He would be paid five dollars and bus fare. After just one game, Reagan's salary doubled to ten dollars a broadcast. He seemed to be on his way. After the final game of the season, however, MacArthur told Reagan the station no longer needed his services. He said he would call if something opened up. With the Great Depression getting worse everyday, Reagan did not expect that to happen. His only job prospect was another summer of lifeguarding.

In February 1933, things suddenly changed for the better. MacArthur called him with a job offer. A staff announcer at WOC had quit. He offered Reagan the job at a salary of one hundred dollars a month. Reagan eagerly accepted. At the age of twenty-two, he was making more money than his father ever had.

By then, Reagan was already planning his next career move. He wanted to act in the movies.

Chapter Two

Sportscaster to Movie Star

Reagan started work at the radio station his first day in Davenport. As an entry-level announcer, he did a little of everything—played records, read commercials, and filled airtime during programming breaks. He discovered that reading commercials was tougher than describing college football. He stumbled over words and his delivery was stiff. "The secret of announcing, is to make reading sound like talking," Reagan wrote. "At that time I was plain awful. I knew it, and so did the listeners. What was worse, so did the sponsors."

Before too long, Reagan was told he was going to be replaced. He would be "kept in mind" for sports broadcasting assignments. When his replacement arrived, Reagan was told to train him. The replacement had been working as a teacher. Reagan told his successor how he had been summarily fired. That worried the replacement, so he asked the station for a contract. If he was going to give up the job security of teaching, he wanted some commitment from WOC. The station refused. The successor quit, and Reagan was rehired.

Reagan began rehearsing commercials, practicing his delivery and working on the rhythm and cadence of his speech. He was soon a polished performer. WOC stopped looking for a replacement.

After a few months at WOC, Reagan was transferred to another station, WHO in Des Moines, Iowa. WHO was building a fifty-thousand-watt transmitter. At that time, there were only about fifteen radio stations in the U.S. with that broadcasting power. Reagan would be working for one of the most powerful National Broadcasting Company (NBC) affiliated stations in America.

Reagan broadcast college football, swimming, and track meets. He became best known for his ability to recreate Chicago Cubs and White Sox baseball games. He sat in a booth and waited for the play-by-play to arrive via telegraph. When there was a delay, he had to improvise. Once, when the wire went dead, he pretended a batter fouled off several pitches. When the wire came back, he learned that the batter had popped up on the first pitch. He had to ad-lib to cover his ad-libs.

Reagan kept busy with sports in his free time as well. A friend had introduced him to horseback riding, and he was hooked. In order to spend more time riding, he joined the cavalry reserve. He also took extension courses in order to qualify for an officer's rank. After two years, he completed his classes and became a second lieutenant in the army reserve, earning an "excel-

As an announcer for the radio station WHO out of Des Moines, Iowa, Ronald Reagan became well known throughout the upper Midwest. (*Courtesy of the Ronald Reagan Library.*)

lent" rating in both character and military efficiency.

Reagan enjoyed working as a sportscaster. After four years at WHO, he made ninety dollars a week, but he was ambitious and wanted more. His dream was to go to Hollywood and act in the movies. He came up with a scheme to pay for a trip to Hollywood.

Both the White Sox and Cubs' spring training camps were in southern California, near Hollywood. Reagan got WHO to pay for a trip to scout the Chicago teams. When he was not broadcasting, he made the rounds at movie studios and talked to agents.

Fortunately, Reagan already had a friend in Hollywood. Actress and singer Joy Hodges had worked with him at WHO. She introduced him to her agent, Bill Meiklejohn, who represented several Hollywood stars, including Robert Taylor, Betty Grable, and Jane Wyman.

Reagan was nearsighted, but Joy told him to get rid of his glasses when he went in for his interview. Reagan sat across the table from Meiklejohn, but could barely see his face. Reagan talked up his acting experience. He fibbed and said that Eureka College Drama Club was a professional acting company. He also claimed that he currently made $180 a week. After awhile, Reagan grew impatient. He bluntly told Meiklejohn: "Look, Joy told me that you would level with me. Should I go back to Des Moines and forget this, or what should I do?"

The agent liked what he saw. Reagan had a handsome, athletic appearance that would appeal to moviegoers. Meiklejohn informed him, "Max is the only casting director in town that has the power to say yes or no." Max Arnow was a casting director at Warner Brothers Studios. Meiklejohn called Arnow to tell him about Reagan. "Max, I have another Robert Taylor sitting in my office." Known as "the man with the perfect face," Robert Taylor was one of Hollywood's most successful leading men.

Max was, of course, skeptical. He was used to hearing agents exaggerate, but he agreed to give Reagan a screen test. He gave him a few pages of script from the play *The Philadelphia Story*. He told Reagan to memorize them and come back in a few days.

Reagan's screen test was short. He and a contract actress from Warner Brothers exchanged a few lines of dialogue. Arnow called Meiklejohn and told him that studio boss Jack Warner would take a look at the test when he could work it into his schedule. The agent told Reagan to stick around California for a few more days.

Reagan astonished both men when he said he could not delay returning to Iowa. "I've got to get back to my job," he said. "The season opener's coming up in a few days and I've got to broadcast the Cubs' games."

He was taking a calculated risk by refusing to change his plans. In his second autobiography, *Ronald Reagan: An American Life*, he said it was a good move. Movie studios were accustomed to people who were desperate for a job. They were taken aback when Reagan told them he would not wait around indefinitely.

Reagan took a train back to Des Moines. Less than forty-eight hours after returning to Iowa, he got a telegram from Meiklejohn. Warner Brothers was offering him a seven-year contract at two hundred dollars a week. Reagan hurried off his reply: "SIGN BEFORE THEY CHANGE THEIR MINDS."

While Reagan attended Eureka College, he once told some classmates his education would be wasted if he were not making five thousand dollars a year five years after graduation. In just under five years from graduation, he was making over twice that salary.

Reagan's contract called for him to start work on June 1, 1937. He stayed at WHO until late May. Then he packed all his possessions into his Nash convertible and headed west. Top down, sun in his face, and wind in his hair, a giddy Ronald Reagan drove to Hollywood.

Before making his first film, Reagan reported to the studio for a Hollywood makeover. He was made aware of all his imperfections. His haircut was wrong; head too small; shoulders too big; and his neck too short. Studio barbers and tailors fixed these "problems."

It was common practice to change young actor's names. (Robert Taylor's real name was Spangler Arlington Brugh.) As a sports broadcaster, he had used the name Dutch Reagan, but that name was unacceptable to Warner Brothers. The studio wanted a name that matched his looks and would be easy to remember.

As they pondered the question, Reagan asked, "How about Ronald?" The makeover people looked at each other and agreed that Ronald Reagan was a pretty good name for an actor. So Dutch Reagan, sportscaster, became Ronald Reagan, actor.

Reagan had not acted since college, and before making his first film, he doubted his talent. He had a seven-year contract, but during the six-month probation period he could be fired for any reason. His insecurity increased when he saw his screen test. He hated it.

Warner Brothers helped Reagan make the transition to movies by giving him the role of a radio announcer in his first film, *Love Is on the Air*. He played a crusading radio announcer who tricks some racketeers into unknowingly confessing their crimes into a live microphone. The trade paper *Hollywood Reporter* gave Reagan a glowing review. "*Love Is on the Air* presents a new leading man, Ronald Reagan, who is a natural, giving one of the best first picture performances Hollywood has offered in many a day."

Over the next four years, Reagan appeared in about twenty movies for Warner Brothers. Practically all of his films were known as "B-movies"—movies that were shot quickly and cheaply and played second in a double feature. Still, he gained valuable acting experience and got to work with some major stars, such as Humphrey Bogart, James Cagney, and Bette Davis.

Of the eight movies Reagan made in 1938, one in particular, *Brother Rat,* would have an impact on his personal life as well as his career. The movie, about a military cadet who romances a commanding officer's daughter, also starred twenty-three-year-old actress Jane Wyman, a beautiful blond starlet who had started her career as a radio singer. Reagan and Wyman began dating and were engaged by the end of filming. Married a year and a half later, they were soon paired in two movies as husband and wife, but neither picture generated enthusiasm and they never acted together again.

In 1940, Reagan got his first role in an "A" feature film. He played Notre Dame football star George Gipp in the movie, *Knute Rockne—All American.* Knute Rockne had been the head football coach at Notre Dame University from 1918 to 1931. He compiled a record of 105 wins, twelve losses, and five ties, won three national championships, and had five undefeated seasons. Rockne's career was cut short in an airplane crash when he was forty-three.

One of Rockne's football players, George Gipp, also died young. Gipp, Notre Dame's first All-American, died of pneumonia. Coach Rockne once used Gipp's reputed dying words to inspire his team to come from behind and win against Army. The phrase, "win one for the Gipper," became an enduring part of college football history.

A former college football player himself, Reagan enjoyed playing George Gipp. He received favorable reviews for his portrayal of the doomed young football star. The role led to other important parts in A-movies. "It was the springboard that bounced me into a wider variety of parts in pictures," Reagan remembered.

In 1941, on her twenty-seventh birthday, Jane gave birth to the couple's first child, a daughter they named Maureen. That same year, Reagan began filming the most memorable movie of his career, *Kings Row.* He played Drake McHugh, a wealthy, small town playboy.

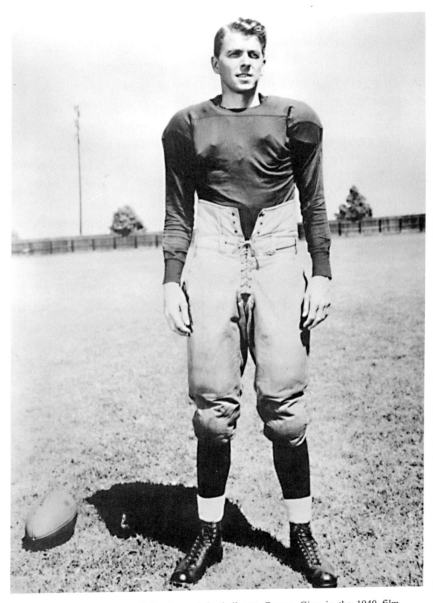

Ronald Reagan portrayed the doomed football star George Gipp in the 1940 film
Knute Rockne—All American. (Courtesy of the Ronald Reagan Library.)

Drake loses his inheritance when the local banker embezzles the funds and is forced to become a railroad laborer. After he is injured at work, a sadistic doctor amputates his legs because of Drake's relationship with his daughter. When he awakens from the surgery and sees what the doctor has done, Reagan delivers his most memorable line as an actor: "Where's the rest of me?" This later became the title of Reagan's first autobiography, published in 1964.

Kings Row was nominated for three Academy Awards and earned Reagan the best reviews of his career. He was on the brink of becoming a major Hollywood star. Unfortunately, outside events interfered. In December 1941, the U.S. entered World War II when the Japanese bombed Pearl Harbor.

Reagan was not immediately inducted (drafted) into the armed forces. When war was declared, he was making a film called *Desperate Journey*, playing the role of an American pilot serving in England's Royal Air Force. Warner Brothers managed to get him a brief draft deferment to complete the movie because it had a patriotic theme. A later request by the studio for a second deferment was denied. On April 14, 1942, Reagan was inducted into the United States Army. Instead of acting for Warner Brothers, he would be making movies for the Army Air Force First Motion Picture Unit.

Chapter Three

Transitions

Because he was a second lieutenant with the army reserve, Reagan entered the army as an officer. Due to his nearsightedness, he was barred from combat duty and spent the war serving in California. His first assignment sent him to Fort Mason in San Francisco. His official position was liaison officer in charge of loading convoys, but the army sent him out to rallies to urge Americans to buy savings bonds and to support the war effort. He also attended charity benefits.

After a few months, Reagan was transferred to the Army Air Force as a member of the Army Air Force First Motion Picture Unit. He narrated recruitment films and training films for bomber pilots.

Reagan had been on active duty for about a year when he was given a furlough in 1943 to appear in a movie version of the Irving Berlin musical, *This Is the Army*. Berlin had persuaded the War Department to give him three hundred servicemen for the project. Profits from the film went to Army Relief, a fund to assist needy soldiers and their families.

During filming, Berlin gave Reagan some praise that flattered and concerned him. Berlin said: "You really should give this business some consideration when the war is over. It's very possible you could have a career in show business." Reagan wondered if Berlin had not seen any of his movies, or if the war had made people forget he was a movie actor.

After Maureen's birth, the Reagans tried to have another child but were unsuccessful. They adopted a baby boy, Michael, in March 1945. Nine months later, on December 9, 1945, Reagan was discharged from the Army Air Force. He was eager to resume his acting career, but the war had undermined his career's momentum. He made twenty-two more movies before retiring, but he never had another success like *Kings Row*.

Stallion Road was Reagan's first movie after leaving the service. He played a veterinarian who perfects a serum that halts an outbreak of anthrax in a herd of cattle. In the process, he becomes infected but recovers when a friend injects him with the untested serum.

By the time the movie was released in March 1947, it had been four years since Reagan had appeared in a movie. Reviews of the film were favorable, but it was not a commercial success. Whatever boost his acting career received from *Stallion Road* was lost by the release of his next film, *That Hagen Girl*. Both movie critics and Reagan agreed it was one of the worst films he had ever made. He played an attorney in love with a

Ronald Reagan and wife Jane Wyman with their two children, Maureen and Michael.
(Courtesy of the Wisconsin Center for Film and Theater Research.)

teenage girl half his age. Former child star Shirley Temple played the title character and Reagan's love interest.

Reagan was also experiencing problems in his private life at this time. *That Hagen Girl* contains a scene in which Temple tries to drown herself in a lake and Reagan dives in to save her. The scene required several takes, and he had to repeatedly jump into the cold water. Six days later, he was hospitalized with pneumonia.

While Reagan was recovering, Jane Wyman was in a different hospital giving birth four months prematurely to a baby girl. The baby survived only twenty-four hours. Wyman had to undergo the ordeal without Reagan there to comfort her.

The couple's relationship was breaking down. The sadness of losing a child, coupled with the strain brought about by his military service, had strained their marriage. In addition, Jane was becoming a successful movie star as Reagan's career was declining. In 1945, she received critical acclaim for her role in *The Lost Weekend*, and the following year she was nominated for an Academy Award for her role in *The Yearling*. Two years later, she won the best actress Academy Award for playing a deaf mute in *Johnny Belinda*.

Another reason for their estrangement was Reagan's increasing involvement with the labor union called the Screen Actors Guild (SAG). In 1947, he was elected president of the union, which consumed more of his time. Conflict developed in his marriage because as Reagan became more politically involved, Jane had no interest in politics. Jane confided to her priest, Father Robert Peralla, "It was exasperating to wake in the middle of the night, prepare for work, and have someone at the breakfast table, newspaper in hand, expounding on the far right, far left, the conservative right, the conservative left, the middle of the roader."

The gossip columnists covered the couple's breakup as avidly as they had their courtship, and although the articles were sympathetic, Reagan was angry at the intrusion into his private life. As he grew older, Reagan kept his personal affairs as private as possible, undoubtedly in reaction to such news coverage.

In February 1948, Jane Wyman announced she was divorcing Reagan. He did not want the marriage to end, and they briefly reconciled, but a divorce decree was finalized in July 1949. Jane was awarded custody of their two children, Maureen and Michael, and five hundred dollars a month for child support.

After he started living alone, Reagan became even more involved in SAG business and politics. Instead of family and filmmaking, union business and politics became the center of his life.

Reagan's movie career was winding down, but his involvement in SAG was directing him towards his next profession—politics.

Chapter Four

Un-American Activities

Following World War II, the United States entered into a long conflict with the Soviet Union, now known as the Cold War. In the years following World War II, the Communist dominated Soviet Union was consolidating its hold over Eastern Europe. Berlin, the former capital of Germany, was divided into two sections, and Soviet and American troops came close to war there several times. The Cold War would cause tumult into the 1990s, when the Soviet Union would finally collapse.

As tensions developed, some Americans feared Communists were infiltrating the U.S. government, armed forces, and entertainment industry. Labor unions attempted to rid their organizations of Communists, while teachers and other government employees were often required to take loyalty oaths. An atmosphere of suspicion and paranoia hung over the nation.

In May 1947, the House Un-American Activities Committee (HUAC), which had been founded to uncover subversive and treasonous individuals and organizations, began investigating "communist infiltration of the motion picture industry." Some on the committee believed Communist directors, producers, and screenwriters were injecting propaganda into movies. When the HUAC held preliminary fact-finding hearings, Reagan traveled to Washington to testify as a friendly witness. In his testimony he stated, "I do not believe that the communists have ever at any time been able to use the motion picture screen as a sounding board for their philosophy or ideology." Reagan acknowledged there was a "small clique" of SAG members who were "suspected of more or less following the tactics that we associate with the Communist Party."

Reagan opposed the ideology of Communism, which called for the end of private property and the market economy. Following rumors of physical threats directed toward him during a movie industry labor strike, Reagan was recruited by the Federal Bureau of Investigation (FBI) to provide the agency with the names of actors and others working in the movie industry whom he suspected of being Communists. Reagan provided the FBI with names for five years, from 1943 to 1947.

One director and nine screenwriters were called to testify before the committee. They refused to reveal their political affiliations or to answer the committee's standard question, "Are you now or have you ever been a member of the Communist Party?" The group became known as the "Hollywood Ten," and in April 1948, they were convicted of contempt of Congress in Federal Court and received the maximum sentence of a year in jail and a one thousand dollar fine. After serving their time, the Hollywood Ten were blacklisted (prevented from working) by the American film industry. They had to work abroad or use pseudonyms (false names).

Reagan's cooperation with the committee hinted at his transition to a conservative Republican. He had been a Democrat since childhood, when his father managed the local welfare office. "Probably because of my dad's influence and my experiences during the Depression, I had loved the Democratic Party," Reagan wrote.

Reagan believed the Democratic Party had changed from the party he remembered. He later wrote:

> Our federal bureaucracy expanded relentlessly during the postwar years . . . Our government was confiscating a disproportionate share of the nation's wealth through excessive taxes, and indirectly seizing control of the day-to-day management of our businesses with rules and regulations that often gave Washington bureaucrats the power of life and death over them.

Throughout the 1940s, however, he continued to support Democratic candidates. In 1948, he campaigned for President Harry S. Truman's re-election. Two years later, he supported Democrat Helen Gahagan Douglas against Richard M. Nixon in the California Senate race.

By 1949, Reagan was spending as much time at the negotiating table for SAG as he was before the movie cameras. When not involved in union activities, he was bickering with Warner Brothers over the roles the studio offered him. On January 6, 1950, Bob Thomas of the *Los Angeles Mirror* interviewed the actor. About his roles, Reagan said: "I'm going to pick my own pictures. I have come to the conclusion that I could do as good a job of picking as the studio has done . . . At least I could do no worse. With the parts that I've had, I could telephone my lines in and it wouldn't make a difference."

To help Reagan gain more control over his career, his agent negotiated a new contract that stipulated Reagan would only have to make one movie a year for Warner Brothers. This left him free to look for other opportunities, but his freedom came with a price—a fifty percent pay cut. A week later, he signed a five-year, five-picture deal with Universal Studios. Although he ended up only making three movies for Universal from 1950 to 1953, he had more input on his roles. He was also able to take roles outside of the movies. On December 7, 1950, he made his first television appearance on the CBS program *Airflyte Theater*.

Busy with union business and movie roles, Reagan did not have much of a social life. He later said of this period, "I was footloose and fancy free, and I guess down underneath, miserable." Then an unexpected call from a movie director changed his life. Mervyn LeRoy was directing a movie titled *East Side, West Side* for MGM Studios. One of his contract actresses, Nancy Davis, was worried about being blacklisted. Apparently, another actress with the same name had been identified as a Communist. LeRoy wanted Reagan to use his influence as the president of SAG to clear her

Ronald Reagan and Nancy Davis were married on March 4, 1952. In this wedding photo, the couple is accompanied by fellow actor William Holden, who served as best man, and Holden's wife, Ardis. (*Courtesy of the Ronald Reagan Library.*)

name. When Reagan agreed to help Nancy Davis, she insisted on a face-to-face meeting.

Reagan called Nancy and asked if she was free for dinner. When she said yes, he explained it would have to be an early dinner because had to get up the next morning to work in a movie. Nancy said that was fine, she was working also. They were both lying. Neither was working at the time, but the ploy gave them an excuse for an early exit if they did not like each other.

Nancy Davis was the daughter of a one-time actress and stepdaughter of a noted Chicago surgeon. Reagan showed up at her apartment that November evening supported by two canes. He had broken his thigh in six places during a charity baseball game and had only recently been released from the hospital, where he spent seven weeks flat on his back. The couple ended up staying out till 3 A.M., and that one date convinced Nancy that Reagan was the man she wanted to marry. "I knew that being his wife was the role I wanted most."

Although Reagan continued to go out with other women for a few weeks, Nancy soon became his "steady." Gossip columnists covered the couple's relationship, but they usually managed to avoid the limelight. After dating for about three years, they were married on March 4, 1952. Ronald was forty-one years old, and Nancy was twenty-eight. On October 22 of that same year, Nancy gave birth to their first child, Patricia Ann.

After she married Reagan, Nancy put his career ahead of hers. She appeared in only three more films. In her final movie, a World War II drama called *Hellcats of the*

Navy, she co-starred with Reagan and played a navy nurse. He played a submarine commander.

Reagan's second marriage was more stable than his first. Nancy apparently did not resent dropping her career in favor of his, or his move toward politics. She could always be counted on for loyal support. However, she never felt that she totally understood her enigmatic husband. Years later she wrote: "There's a wall around him. He lets me come closer than anyone else, but there are times when even I feel that barrier."

In 1954, Reagan had to supplement his movie income by performing with a male quartet called The Continentals at nightclubs in Los Angeles and Las Vegas. He sang, told jokes, did some slapstick comedy, and then closed the act by reciting a poem about the life of an actor. Although the show received good reviews and an offer for more engagements, Reagan refused. It was the lowest point of his show business career.

Reagan's movie career was declining while television was stealing an increasingly larger slice of the audience. In 1948, only one percent of American homes had a television set. By 1953, the number had leapt to fifty percent. During the 1950s, returning soldiers settled down, started families, and joined the work force. Family life centered on the home, and many evenings were spent watching television. Veteran movie stars looked down on the industry, but Reagan did not have that luxury. He knew his best movie roles were behind him. Television would not only revitalize Reagan's acting career, it would launch his political career.

Chapter Five

Politics and Television

Reagan made guest appearances on several television shows. He had resigned as president of the Screen Actors Guild in November 1952 and had more time to work. The movie roles were drying up, and when he was offered a television series in 1954, he accepted it. The General Electric Corporation (GE) was looking for a well-known actor to host their weekly television series. He was also expected to act as corporate spokesman, appear in commercials, give speeches, and greet executives and employees at plants. His salary was $125,000 a year plus payments for acting in the episodes and for touring the plants. *General Electric Theater* was broadcast on Sunday evenings on CBS. Each episode featured a guest star in a role ranging from light comedy to serious melodrama.

Six years into his second marriage, when their daughter Patti was five, Nancy gave birth to Ronald Prescott Reagan on May 20, 1958. The growing family lived in a home overlooking the ocean. This "house of the future" was jam-packed with GE appliances and gadgets.

During his eight years as host of *General Electric Theater*, Reagan acted in thirty-five episodes. Nancy co-starred in three. Besides providing him with a high salary, the series kept Reagan in the public eye. For five-and-a-half years, October 1955 to April 1961, *General Electric Theater* was one of the top rated shows. The job helped Reagan hone his speaking skills. He visited all of the company's 135 plants and later estimated that he personally met 250,000 employees and spent over four thousand hours making speeches, sometimes as many as fourteen in one day.

His speeches reached a wider audience than just GE employees. Reagan spoke to civic clubs, such as the Lions, Kiwanis, Elks, Rotary Club, and the American Legion. The speeches addressed the concerns of most Americans—taxes, crime, juvenile delinquency, and the need for strong families and wholesome values.

As GE's spokesperson, Reagan began to clarify his own political beliefs. Often his speeches were followed by a question-and-answer session. Many of the questions concerned politics and economic policy. Reagan usually defended corporations and attacked government regulation, a position associated with the Republican Party. Reagan's role at GE confirmed him as a defender of big business. Although still a registered Democrat, Reagan supported the Republican candidate Dwight D. Eisenhower for president in 1952. Four years later, he supported Eisenhower's bid for re-election.

When Republican Vice President Richard M. Nixon ran for president against Massachusetts Senator John F. Kennedy in 1960, Reagan decided it was time to change parties. However, Nixon, who was also from California, convinced him to wait until after the election. It was decided that Reagan would be more effective campaigning for Nixon if he remained a Democrat. Reagan made over two hundred campaign speeches in support of Nixon. "I literally traveled the same kind of campaign route the candidate himself traveled—all over the country," Reagan said.

Reagan's active partisanship began to make his bosses at GE uncomfortable. They did not want to appear to be taking sides in elections. Reagan also discovered GE did not think all government spending and regulation was a bad thing. When he attacked the Tennessee Valley Authority (TVA) as an example of wasteful government spending, GE decided it was time to intervene. The TVA had been started during the Depression to build dams. It brought electricity to thousands of poor people in the southern states who had no other way to receive it. TVA also spent fifty million dollars a year buying equipment from GE. Reagan stopped attacking the TVA after GE President Ralph Cordiner told him, "It would make my job easier."

In 1962, Reagan's contract with GE was up for renewal, but the popularity of *General Electric Theater* had declined. The western series *Bonanza* had the same Sunday night time slot and consistently drew a larger audience. Also, GE's discomfort with the political tone

Ronald Reagan, wife Nancy, and their two children, Patti and Ronald Jr., in 1960.
(*Courtesy of the Ronald Reagan Library.*)

of Reagan's speeches had increased after the election of Democratic President John F. Kennedy.

The 1960s were a period of social upheaval that focused on the battle for civil rights, the developing war in Vietnam, and near nuclear war with the Soviet Union over Cuba. Reagan's rhetoric became harsher, as he had little respect for the new president or his policies. He believed Kennedy was soft on Communism. He feared the country was drifting toward socialism and that welfare and other social programs drained individual initiative. He made these points in his speeches, and according to one GE executive, he was the most popular public speaker in America, with the exception of former President Eisenhower.

The tension between Reagan and GE's management climaxed when an executive told him to limit speeches to the selling of GE products. Reagan refused. "There's no way that I could go out now to an audience that is expecting the type of thing that I've been doing for the last eight years and suddenly stand up and start selling them electric toasters," Reagan said. "That's it. If it's the speeches, then you only have one choice. Either I don't do the speeches at all for you, or we don't do the program; you get somebody else." Within forty-eight hours, GE had canceled the show. Reagan was unemployed and free to make all the speeches he wanted.

Reagan did not have to worry about money. He was in high demand as a speaker and even landed a few acting roles. In 1963 and 1964, he appeared in two television shows—*Wagon Train* and *Kraft Suspense Theater*. He also appeared in his fifty-third, and final, film.

Originally made for television, *The Killers* was considered too violent and was released in movie theaters. For the only time in his career, Reagan played a villain. He was not comfortable with the part and regretted making the movie. He preferred playing the good guy.

Reagan, now a registered Republican, was in his early fifties. After three decades, his acting career was over. He had, however, become influential in the Republican Party. In 1964, Arizona Senator Barry Goldwater was nominated as the Republican candidate to run against the Democratic incumbent, President Lyndon B. Johnson. Johnson had become president after President Kennedy was assassinated on November 22, 1963.

Goldwater was a surprise winner of the Republican nomination after a bitter series of primaries. Representing the most conservative wing of the Republican Party, he defeated the favored candidate, New York Governor Nelson Rockefeller. Many Republicans, particularly from the South and West, had felt shut out of the Republican Party for years. They believed the party was controlled by Wall Street and the wealthy establishment in the Northeast. In the 1960s, as the Democratic Party became more aligned with the Civil Rights Movement, many white Southerners became Republicans, and the Republican Party power base shifted from the Northeast to the South and the West. These were Goldwater's most active supporters as he spoke out against the federal government. He advocated a much fiercer war in Vietnam and opposed federal welfare programs.

Reagan served as the co-chairman of the California Republicans for Goldwater committee. He made speeches, raised money, and throughout the campaign delivered his standard speech, attacking Democrats and government bureaucrats. He always concluded the speech by saying Americans had a choice—continue on the current path, or fight to reclaim liberties he said had been taken away by the federal government.

In late summer 1964, Reagan delivered his speech to an audience of around eight hundred party faithful at the Coconut Grove Nightclub in Los Angeles. Afterward, a small group of big Republican contributors asked Reagan to give the speech on national television. He said he would if they thought it would help. Goldwater was trailing badly in the polls.

The speech was broadcast on October 27, 1964, a week before election day. "A Time for Choosing," was essentially his GE speech. He used quotes from James Madison, Alexander Hamilton, and Karl Marx to denounce Communism and government waste, while praising individual freedom. He ended the speech by saying: "You and I have a rendezvous with destiny [a phrase taken from Franklin D. Roosevelt]. We can preserve for our children this the last best hope of man on earth or we can sentence them to take the first step into a thousand years of darkness. If we fail, at least let our children and our children's children, say of us we justified our brief moment here. We did all that could be done."

The televised address was a huge success and raised around one million dollars, but it was too late to help Goldwater. In spite of the last minute contributions generated by the speech, the election went as expected. President Johnson carried forty-four out of fifty states and received sixty-one percent of the popular vote. The Democrats also picked up enough seats in the House and Senate to have two-to-one majorities in both houses of Congress.

A disaster for the Republican Party, the 1964 election was a significant milestone for Reagan's political career. In California, Republican George Murphy, a former movie actor, was elected to the U.S. Senate.

Ronald Reagan campaigned for Barry Goldwater, the 1964 Republican presidential candidate. (*Courtesy of the Library of Congress.*)

Murphy's election showed Reagan an actor could get elected to high political office. The overwhelming defeat also ended Barry Goldwater's reign as the leading spokesman for Republican conservatives. This paved the way for Reagan to become the top spokesman and fund-raiser for the conservative wing of the party.

Two months after Goldwater's defeat, a group of wealthy California Republicans met at the home of Holmes P. Tuttle. Tuttle owned several Ford dealerships in the Los Angeles area. He had been a major fundraiser and powerful figure among California Republicans since the early 1950s. Tuttle and his friends decided to approach Reagan and ask him to run for governor of California in the 1966 election.

In February 1965, Holmes and two associates, Cy Rubel, former head of the Union Oil Company, and Henry Salvatori, another wealthy businessman, called on Reagan and asked him to run for governor. Initially, Reagan refused, but the three backers were persistent. Finally, Reagan said he would think it over. Then, without waiting for a commitment from Reagan, Tuttle went to the political consulting firm of Spencer-Roberts. "We checked with people around the country, and they said that Spencer-Roberts was the best," Tuttle explained. "We didn't want anything less than the best." The firm balked at the idea of Reagan for governor. "We had reservations about Reagan," Bill Roberts said. "We had heard that Reagan was a real right-winger and we thought that a right-wing kind of candidacy would not be a successful one."

After meeting with Reagan, Roberts changed his mind. He found Reagan to be "an open and candid person, easy to talk with, and a good listener." Roberts was also encouraged by Tuttle's commitment to raise as much money as was needed to get Reagan elected.

In the late spring of 1965, Roberts and Tuttle formed an organization called "Friends of Ronald Reagan" and began raising money. Although he claimed he had not yet made up his mind, Reagan now had an organization and money. The only thing left to do was announce his candidacy.

Chapter Six

Governor Reagan

On January 4, 1966, Reagan formally announced his candidacy for the Republican California gubernatorial nomination. The announcement was a combination television appearance, press conference, and public reception. During the press conference, there were the expected questions about his lack of political experience. Reagan had been well prepared for them. He presented himself as an outsider who was running as a concerned citizen. "As I have stated, I am not a politician in the sense of ever having held public office. I think I can qualify as a citizen-politician and I don't believe that this country was created by men who were politicians."

The incumbent governor, Democrat Edmund "Pat" Brown, was seeking a third four-year term. Governor Brown felt a retired movie actor was not much of a threat. In 1958, he had defeated William F. Knowland, a popular U.S. senator, and in 1962 he ended former Vice President Richard Nixon's bid for a political comeback after losing the 1960 presidential campaign to Kennedy. Brown thought Reagan's opponent for the Republican nomination, former San Francisco Mayor George Christopher, would be the Republican nominee. Years later Brown said: "I thought it was a joke. I really felt that running a motion picture actor—and one who was not a grade A actor at that—was so funny I didn't regard Ronald Reagan as a strong candidate."

Governor Brown began taking Reagan seriously after the Republican primary, when the former actor defeated Christopher by a two-to-one margin—1,417,623 votes to 675,683. A decisive victory in a primary makes it easier for a party to unite behind a candidate. In contrast, Governor Brown won his primary with just fifty-two percent of the vote. The remainder was divided among five other opponents. The narrow win and the crowded field of candidates meant the Democrats would be less unified than the Republicans.

Some of Reagan's campaign attacks against Governor Brown were identical to those that would be used in future elections. He attacked his "failed leadership" and blamed Governor Brown for high state taxes, the increasing costs of welfare benefits, and student unrest on California university campuses.

Governor Brown fought back by highlighting Reagan's lack of political experience and his background as a movie actor. He repeatedly told voters, "Reagan is only an actor who memorizes speeches written by other people, just like he memorized lines that were fed to him by screenwriters in the movies."

The image of Reagan as an actor with no thoughts or ideas of his own initially worked to Brown's advantage. Reagan realized he had to change that image. He met with his campaign managers and asked to meet with the voters. They were opposed to this tactic. In the heat of a campaign, or in an unguarded moment, even an experienced candidate could say something he would later regret. This was Reagan's first run for office, but he was confident the people could tell the difference between a programmed response and a thoughtful answer. Against the advice of his managers, Reagan began to travel around the state giving short talks and answering questions. The experience was similar to his days of speaking and meeting employees at GE.

Reagan's decision to take questions from the audience was a success. He began to climb in the polls. On November 8, 1966, he stunned most political observers by winning fifty-eight percent of the vote. The former actor was the new governor of California.

As he prepared to take office, Reagan made an unpleasant discovery. He would be entering office with a two hundred million dollar budget deficit. Governor Brown, in order to avoid a tax increase in an election year, had changed the state's accounting system so revenues were counted when they became collectible, but before they were actually received. In the past, revenues were counted only when they were collected.

Reagan was sworn in as California's governor, with Nancy standing proudly by his side. The ceremony took place at two minutes after midnight on January 2,

California Governor-elect Reagan takes the oath of office in a private ceremony in 1967. (*Courtesy of the Ronald Reagan Library.*)

1967, beneath the golden dome of the capitol building. In his inaugural speech, Reagan called the accounting changes made by Brown, "a gimmick that solved nothing but only postponed the day of reckoning." Without going into specifics, he pledged a frugal administration: "We are going to squeeze and cut and trim until we reduce the cost of government. It won't be easy, nor will it be pleasant, and it will involve every department of government starting with the governor's office."

Reagan wanted to balance the state budget without raising taxes. In an attempt to do so, he ordered all agencies to cut their budgets by ten percent and instituted a hiring freeze. When an employee resigned or retired, no replacement was supposed to be hired.

Within six weeks, Reagan had learned his first lesson about governing—it is easier to give orders than it is to have them enacted. Most agencies said it was not possible for them to carry out their jobs, provide the services that the legislature had mandated they provide, and cut their budgets ten percent. If Reagan wanted to make these cuts, he would have to ask the legislature to tell the agencies where to cut back. Reagan knew the legislature was not willing to do this and had no choice but to submit another budget without the promised cuts. The revised budget totaled $440 million more than the initial budget, and he had to suffer the embarrassment of sending the California Assembly the biggest budget in the state's history.

Reagan's power as governor was limited. His popularity did not help other Republican candidates in 1966, and the Democrats controlled both houses of the California Assembly. The Democratic speaker of the Assembly, Jesse Unruh, was able to block legislation. California newspapers called Speaker Unruh, not Governor Reagan, "the state's most powerful politician."

The political battles pitted a novice governor against an experienced legislator. Despite their political differences, Reagan developed a respect for his opponent. "Over time, I gained some grudging respect for Unruh's skills as a legislative tactician," Reagan said. "He was good at what he did—but he put partisanship above all else." Reagan worked with Unruh to enact an increase in the state income tax to balance the budget. Reagan also signed a bill legalizing abortion in the cases of rape and incest or to protect the woman's life.

At the end of Reagan's first legislative season, he and Nancy threw a party for his staff. As the staff and their families stood around the pool at the Reagans' home, a little girl fell into the water and sank to the bottom. No one noticed except Reagan, who quickly jumped in to rescue her. After he had placed her on the edge of the pool, he could say he had rescued seventy-eight people from drowning.

In the spring of 1967, some of his backers urged him to run for the Republican presidential nomination. At that time, the two leading contenders were New York Governor Nelson Rockefeller and Michigan Governor George Romney. Former Vice President Richard Nixon was not regarded as a serious candidate because of his defeat in the 1962 California governor's race. After that loss, Nixon gave a news conference and announced his retirement from politics with the words "You [reporters] won't have Dick Nixon to kick around" any longer. Reagan's backers felt they could count on the support of the national party's conservatives. He allowed his backers to proceed but thought their timing was not right. "My feeling was that to go straight from Hollywood to governor and one year after you were there to be in a position of saying, 'I want to be President of the United States,' there was no way I could do that and be credible."

Reagan refused to enter any of the state primary elections that usually decide the party's nominee. Nixon, however, did enter and surprisingly won most. Reagan received 182 delegate votes at the convention, but Nixon won the nomination on the first ballot.

In November 1968, Nixon narrowly defeated the Democratic nominee, Vice President Hubert Humphrey. Nixon's victory freed Reagan to seek a second term as governor. It was widely assumed Nixon would serve two terms. Four more years as governor of the nation's most populous state would put Reagan in a position to run for president in 1976.

Reagan's first term and his re-election bid took place during a turbulent time. Martin Luther King Jr. and Robert Kennedy were assassinated. Racial conflict turned deadly in many cities, including Los Angeles. As the Vietnam War escalated, the protest movement dominated university campuses. At the 1968 Democratic national convention in Chicago, police attacked anti-war protestors with guns and tear gas. In 1970, the year of Reagan's re-election, national guardsmen shot and killed four students at Kent State University in Ohio.

California was the center of much of the anti-war movement. Reagan had campaigned in 1966 against the "hippies" and "communists" in the university system, particularly at the University of California at Berkeley. He kept up the pressure as governor. He had the state university system president fired because he did not think he was tough enough on the protestors. As the campus unrest escalated, Reagan continued to speak out. "No one is compelled to attend the university," he said at one point. "Those who do attend should accept and obey the prescribed rules, or pack up and get out."

In his 1970 campaign for a second term, Reagan opposed his old legislative nemesis. Jesse Unruh blamed Reagan for higher taxes, rising welfare costs, increases in crime, and student disorders and demonstrations at California universities. A *Life* magazine article summed up the situation: "Reagan has failed almost completely to keep his California campaign promises of 1966—the costs of welfare and higher education has risen hideously, California campuses have remained battlegrounds and his 'tax reform' program has been turned down in the legislature. But he neither hides these embarrassments or wastes a moment explaining—as he has every right to do—that many of them stem from inflation and other forces beyond his control."

In the final weeks of the campaign, Unruh gained in the polls. Reagan responded by calling Unruh "a demagogue," "a hypocrite," "dishonest," and "a man who has no regard for the truth."

In 1968, the Democratic convention in Chicago, Illinois, erupted into a conflict between anti-Vietnam War protesters and the Chicago police. (*AP Photo.*)

Reagan won the election, but it was a tighter margin than in 1966. He received fifty-two percent of the vote, way down from the fifty-eight percent margin in 1966. This weaker showing drained his influence in the California Assembly.

In his second term, Reagan concentrated on welfare reform. During his first term, the number of welfare recipients had more than doubled. He had a plan to reform the system, but it required strong bipartisan support. A new assembly speaker, Bob Moretti, did not like Reagan, and he knew Reagan felt the same about him. That did not keep them from working together, however. "I shared an image of him as a pitch man who was a good communicator, who was more interested in selling himself and his administration than he was in accomplishment," Moretti said of Reagan. "But he was the governor and it was get together or do nothing."

When they met, Moretti said: "Look governor, I don't like you particularly, and I know that you don't like me, but we don't have to be in love to work together. If you're serious about doing some things, then let's sit down and start doing it." They passed the California Welfare Reform Act, which tightened eligibility requirements for welfare recipients and reduced the number of hours a father could work before his family became ineligible for benefits. It also required recipients to live in California for one year before they could receive benefits. In three years, 275,000 recipients were dropped from California's welfare roles. Although a bipartisan effort, voters gave Reagan most of the credit.

Chapter Seven

Campaigning for President

Ronald Reagan did not run for a third term in 1974. He was succeeded in 1975 by Jerry Brown, the son of the man he had defeated in 1966. He had been "bookended" by two liberal Democrats from the same family. It was a sign of the times. The Republican Party had fallen to the lowest point in its history; some commentators were even saying it was time to form a new conservative party.

The decline in the fortunes of the Republican Party culminated in the resignation of President Nixon in August 1974 because of his involvement in the Watergate scandal. After protesting for two years that he knew nothing about a June 1972 break-in at the Democratic Party headquarters, located in the Watergate Hotel in Washington, D.C., Nixon had finally been forced to release a series of tapes that made it clear he had been involved in covering up the crime from the beginning. In the 1974 midterm elections, which occurred

The 1974 resignation of President Richard M. Nixon created a crisis of confidence within the Republican Party. (*AP Photo.*)

only weeks after Nixon's resignation, the Republicans lost forty-three seats in the House, four in the Senate, and four governorships. A 1975 poll revealed that only eighteen percent of voters identified themselves as Republicans, and that most Americans thought the Republican Party was untrustworthy, incompetent, and too closely aligned with big business.

Ironically, the bad times probably worked to Reagan's advantage. He had been safely away in California during the Watergate scandal. After leaving the governor's office, he began a nationally syndicated radio show that was broadcast on over two hundred stations. He wrote a column that appeared in 174 newspapers and made eight to ten speeches a month.

Although he enjoyed politics and believed his ideas were what the country needed, Reagan always appeared to be a reluctant candidate. After eight years as governor earning a limited salary, he did enjoy making more money as a political commentator and public speaker. Running for president would mean a cut in pay. The idea of settling down at the ranch he had recently bought and influencing public policy through the media did have its appeal. His ambition, however, was not to be denied. On November 20, 1975, Reagan announced he would challenge President Gerald R. Ford for the Republican presidential nomination.

After Nixon's resignation, President Ford was technically the incumbent, but he entered the 1976 presidential campaign in a particularly weak position. For the first time in history, the president had never been on

Gerald Ford, who became president after Richard M. Nixon resigned because of the Watergate scandal, is the only person to become president without running in a national election. (*Courtesy of the Gerald R. Ford Library.*)

a national ticket. Ford had become vice president after Vice President Spiro Agnew was forced to resign because of corruption he had taken part in while serving as governor of Maryland. Nixon had selected Ford to replace Agnew, and he had been approved by the Congress as directed by the Twenty-fifth Amendment to the Constitution. When Nixon resigned, Ford then became president. One month later, Ford granted Nixon a "full, free and absolute pardon," for any crimes he may have committed. The pardoning of Nixon undercut Ford's popularity.

Ford added to his problems in the Republican Party when he appointed former New York Governor Nelson Rockefeller to fill his recently vacated position as vice president. Conservative Republicans had long considered Rockefeller to be too liberal. These same conservatives were enthusiastic when Reagan challenged Ford.

Reagan's run for the nomination got off to a bad start. He lost the first five primaries, and after only a month, the campaign was two million dollars in debt. Prominent Republicans began calling for Reagan to quit the race in the interest of party unity. Reagan responded that he would not stop campaigning until he had made it to the Republican convention in Kansas City.

The next primary was in North Carolina. Despite his brave words, this was a must-win for Reagan. He was supported by the conservative Republican Senator Jesse Helms, who worked hard to line up votes for Reagan.

Up until this point in the race, Reagan had followed

what he called the eleventh commandment: "Thou shall not speak ill of a fellow Republican." In North Carolina, he began to violate this rule. An unexpected one hundred thousand dollar loan allowed the Reagan campaign to buy television time to broadcast a thirty-minute Reagan speech denouncing the national defense policies of Ford and his secretary of state, Henry Kissinger, on fifteen North Carolina television stations.

The Republicans in North Carolina gave Reagan his first primary win. It was a critical turning point in the campaign and in Reagan's career. He went from looking like a loser to posing a serious challenge to a sitting president. He went on to win primaries in Texas, Alabama, Georgia, and California. Ford countered with wins in Michigan, Ohio, and New Jersey. By mid-July, the race was a dead heat. Neither candidate had enough delegates to win the nomination on the first ballot, although a poll in the *Washington Post* gave Ford a slender lead of 1,093 delegates to Reagan's 1,030. A total of 1,130 votes was needed. To win, Reagan would have to get three-fourths of the uncommitted delegates. This was considered unlikely, and many Republicans were ready to declare Ford the winner.

Reagan took a major gamble to keep the race going into the convention. On July 26, days before the convention opened, he announced liberal Senator Richard S. Schweiker of Pennsylvania would be his running mate. The announcement was unprecedented. A vice-presidential candidate had never been named before the presidential candidate was chosen. Reagan was hoping Senator Schweiker could deliver Pennsylvania's ninety-six uncommitted delegates.

The early selection of a liberal senator may have backfired. Several Southern delegates turned to Ford, and Schweiker did not have enough influence to deliver Pennsylvania's uncommitted delegates. By announcing his choice for vice president, Reagan did manage to remain in the limelight. Ford could not win until the Pennsylvania delegates' votes were counted.

All the maneuvering focused attention on the Republican convention in Kansas City. Ford won the nomination on the first ballot. In his concession speech, Reagan did not mention the president. Instead, he made it clear that he planned to run again. He finished by quoting some lines from the British poet John Dryden. "Lay me down and bleed a while," Reagan said. "Though I am wounded, I am not slain. I shall rise and fight again."

Despite his avowed support for Ford, Reagan campaigned very little for him in his race against the Democratic candidate, former Georgia Governor Jimmy Carter. Although he hit the campaign trail to stump for conservative Republican congressional candidates, during the final week of the campaign Reagan even declined to travel with Ford in California. He sent the president a telegram explaining that he had other obligations.

Ford was able to carry California and twenty-six other states, but Carter won both the electoral vote, 297 to 240, and the popular vote, receiving a little over 40.8

million of approximately eighty million votes cast. The big surprise was not that Carter had won, but that Ford had come so close to holding on to the White House. All factors had made 1976 look like a strong Democratic year.

Later, some Ford supporters were bitter that Reagan had not worked harder to help Ford. They thought he had not wanted Ford to win so he would have a clear path to the nomination in 1980. Reagan supporters, however, pointed out that until the Republican primaries, when he had to fight off Reagan's challenge, Ford was unprepared to run against Carter. Ford had never run in a national election, and had it not been for the opportunity to improve his campaign skills and staff, he would not have made as good a showing as he did. Ford advanced from a thirty percentage point deficit to within two percentage points on election day.

Carter's close victory, and his own strong showing against Ford, set the stage for Reagan to run again in 1980. Beginning in 1977, he traveled across America making speeches supporting conservative causes and candidates. His nationally syndicated radio show and newspaper column continued to keep him in the public eye and earned him a substantial income.

However, Reagan's supporters were concerned about his age. If elected in 1980, he would be sixty-nine when inaugurated, making him America's oldest president. William Henry Harrison had been sixty-eight when he was inaugurated, but he died in office thirty-one days later. Dwight D. Eisenhower served as president when he was in his late sixties, but he suffered a serious heart attack and a briefly disabling stroke while in office. Reagan's relatively youthful appearance helped to deflect the age issue somewhat. His hair was still thick and dark with barely a hint of gray. He did not smoke and he rarely drank. His face had fewer wrinkles than most men his age. He was still a ruggedly handsome man.

Shortly after the 1976 election, Reagan used one million dollars in leftover campaign funds to establish a political action committee called Citizens For The Republic (CFTR). If there had been any doubt that he would run in 1980, this action dispelled them. By law, the one million dollars belonged to Reagan. If he had planned to retire, he could have kept the money.

Throughout 1977, CFTR sent out newsletters pushing Reagan's conservative views to members and potential contributors. The newsletters helped to retain the support of conservatives. CFTR's staff would become the nucleus of the 1980 Reagan campaign team.

During the 1978 congressional elections, both Reagan and Ford hit the campaign trail. Reagan did not expect Ford to seek the presidency in 1980, but he was worried about Ford's continued popularity. Polls showed Ford was the preferred candidate among the Republicans. The former president encouraged journalists to write stories suggesting he would run again.

On November 13, 1979, Reagan formally announced his candidacy. Once again, his campaign did not get off to a smooth start. The first battle for delegates was the

Iowa precinct caucuses in January 1980. Instead of holding a statewide primary, the caucuses were a series of meetings held at the same time all over the state.

A pre-election poll conducted by the Des Moines newspaper gave Reagan fifty percent of the vote. His nearest opponent, former Texas Congressman George Bush, had fourteen percent. The rest of the votes were divided among a crowded field of five other candidates. This optimistic poll may have made Reagan's campaign team a bit too confident. Although Reagan traveled eight times to Iowa, he only visited briefly. Bush would remind Iowa voters he had spent many days in their state while Reagan had only stayed a few hours. Reagan also refused to appear in a debate with Bush and the other candidates—John Connally, Howard Baker, John Anderson, Philip Crane, and Bob Dole.

The Iowa vote was a rude awakening for Reagan and his staff. Bush received 2,182 more votes than Reagan, as well as thirty-three percent of the delegates. Reagan got thirty percent of the delegates. Bush left Iowa bragging he had momentum on his side.

Reagan changed his style of campaigning for the New Hampshire primary. He crisscrossed the tiny state by bus, instead of flying in and out. He worked weekends. Another change in New Hampshire was that he openly attacked Bush for his earlier support of legalizing abortion and for women's rights. New Hampshire Republican voters responded by giving Reagan a convincing win. Bush gamely fought back and scored primary wins in Massachusetts, Connecticut, and Pennsylvania, but narrowly lost to Reagan in his adopted home state of Texas. On May 26, Bush withdrew from the race. Reagan won twenty-eight of the thirty-four Republican presidential primaries.

When the Republicans met in Detroit on July 14, the only unfinished business was the selection of a vice-presidential candidate. The likeliest choice was Bush, but one day later, key Reagan and Ford supporters met quietly to discuss a surprise "dream ticket" of Reagan and Ford. In his autobiography *An American Life*, Reagan wrote he was in favor of selecting Ford as his running mate until he saw CBS newsman Walter Cronkite interview the former president. Ford told Cronkite: "I would not go to Washington and be a figurehead vice president. I would have to be there in the belief that I would play a meaningful role." During a later interview, Ford added that serving under Reagan would require a "far different structure" than had existed before.

Reagan did not want Ford to be a co-president. He wanted a loyal subordinate. It also bothered him that Ford publicly discussed the offer. "I never envisioned him sharing in decisions and wouldn't have accepted it if that had been proposed to me," Reagan wrote.

Around 9:15 on the evening of July 16, Reagan called Ford and asked him to decide if he wanted the vice-presidential nomination. The roll call of states had begun and convention delegates were already casting their votes. About two hours later, Ford turned it down. According to Reagan, Ford simply said, "Look, this isn't gonna work."

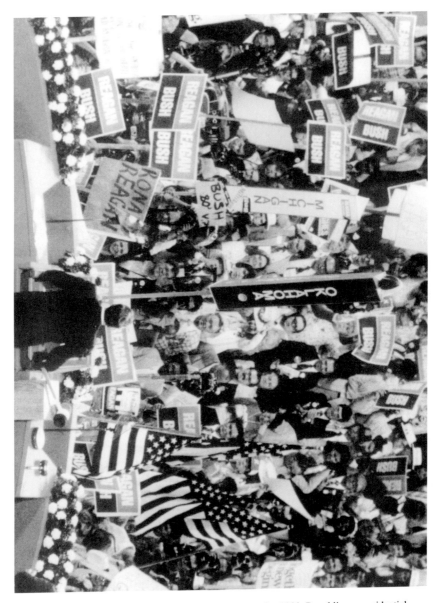

Former California Governor Ronald Reagan won the 1980 Republican presidential nomination on the first ballot. Here he is giving his acceptance speech at the Republican convention in Detroit, Michigan. (*Courtesy of the Ronald Reagan Library.*)

The idea of a Reagan-Ford presidency was intriguing, but the two men never felt comfortable in one another's company. Ford seemed willing to forgive Reagan for attempting to wrest the nomination away from him four years earlier, but he was not able to develop any sense of personal connection to the former governor. "I tried to get to know Reagan, but I failed. I never knew what he was really thinking behind that winning smile," he said.

Within five minutes of Ford's rejection, Reagan called Bush to offer him the vice-presidential nomination. He said: "George, it seems to me that the fellow who came the closest and got the next most votes for president ought to be the logical choice for vice president. Will you take it?" Bush accepted without hesitation. That evening, he was introduced to the convention's delegates as Reagan's running mate. After introducing Bush, Reagan delivered his acceptance speech. Reagan did not just address those at the convention, but also the voters watching on television. He spoke of traditional values such as "family, work, neighborhood, peace and freedom" in an attempt to bring conservative Democrats, independents, and Republicans together to support him. He pledged to build up the military while cutting taxes and balancing the budget. Reagan also attacked what he called "the mediocre leadership" of Jimmy Carter's administration and blamed him for a faltering economy, a weakened defense, and a nationwide energy crisis.

Chapter Eight

Second Try

Jimmy Carter faced many difficulties during his presidency in the last years of the 1970s. The economy, which had grown through the 1960s, weakened throughout the decade, and there were periods of high unemployment. In the past, when jobs were scarce, the inflation rate remained low because people did not spend much money to buy goods, thereby keeping prices from rising. But in the 1970s, a series of oil embargoes imposed by the oil producing countries of the Middle East resulted in rapid increases in the price of oil products. This set off price increases in other manufactured goods. At the same time, interest rates rose.

Although these economic problems had existed under Ford, they continued to grow worse under Carter. Oil embargoes created long gas lines and high heating oil prices. The budget deficit reached $59.9 billion by 1980, a historical high. Democrats and Republicans complained of Carter's indecision. At the beginning of the 1980 campaign, his approval rating was twenty-one percent—the lowest approval rating ever received by a president, including Nixon before he resigned.

Carter did have a historic foreign policy success, but it was soon overshadowed by an embarrassing setback. The success came in 1978 when Egyptian President Anwar Sadat and Israeli Prime Minister Menachem Begin signed a peace agreement in Washington. The Camp David Accords, named for the presidential retreat where most of the negotiations took place, was the first ever peace settlement between an Arab nation and Israel.

The Middle East was also where Carter suffered his biggest disappointment. In November 1979, Iranian students, followers of the Ayatollah Khomeini, stormed the American Embassy in the capital city of Tehran. Months before, Khomeini had forced the ruling shah of Iran out of power and into exile in the United States. The students held fifty-two American Embassy workers hostage. At first, Carter thought he could quickly bring the crisis to an end, but six months later, the hostages were still being held. President Carter then sent a military force to Iran to free them. The mission failed after three helicopters malfunctioned and eight U.S. servicemen died. Carter's inability to negotiate a settlement to the crisis, or to execute a military solution, undercut support for his foreign policy and convinced many Americans he was an ineffective leader. The hostages were held throughout the 1980 presidential election.

Carter's leadership failures had created divisions within the Democratic Party. He was challenged for the

Democratic nomination by Massachusetts Senator Ted
Kennedy, brother of former President John F. Kennedy,
and Governor Jerry Brown of California. While Brown
failed to win any primaries and dropped out on April 1,
1980, Kennedy stunned Carter with a decisive win in
the New York primary. He later won in the populous
states of California and Pennsylvania. Although Carter
still had enough delegates to win on the first ballot at
the Democratic National Convention in August, Kennedy
continued to divide the party by refusing to concede.
He fought for the nomination on the floor by attempting to convince delegates pledged to Carter to change
their votes. When this failed, Kennedy announced he
was no longer a candidate but still insisted Carter support his positions.

Although Carter was a weakened candidate, Reagan's
election was not guaranteed. He had antagonized many
Americans with statements that seemed extreme and
were perceived as too conservative to appeal to a wide
range of voters. It was possible that people would rather
have four more years of Carter than take a risk with
Reagan. His age was also an issue. A poll in *Newsweek*
had Reagan leading Carter by only four percent three
weeks before the election, compared to a twenty-eight
percent lead when he was nominated in July.

Carter fought a hard campaign. When Reagan attacked his record, Carter responded in kind. He emphasized Reagan's inexperience in foreign policy and his
stance against signing a treaty with the Soviet Union to
limit nuclear weapons. He questioned whether Reagan

President Jimmy Carter (center) with Egyptian President Anwar Sadat (left) and Israeli Prime Minister Menachem Begin (right) at the 1978 signing of the historic Camp David Peace Accords between Egypt and Israel. (*Courtesy of the Jimmy Carter Library.*)

would attack and invade other nations without provocation and criticized his earlier refusal to support civil rights legislation, such as the 1964 Civil Rights Act and the 1965 Voting Rights Act. Carter emphasized his support for an amendment to the U.S. Constitution guaranteeing women's rights, his support of legalized abortion, and his support for affirmative action for minorities and Reagan's opposition to all three.

Throughout the campaign, Reagan and Carter had avoided meeting each other in a face-to-face debate. At first, Reagan's advisors did not think he needed to debate Carter. However, with election day drawing near and Carter closing the gap, Reagan agreed to a single nationally televised debate.

During the debate, held on October 28, 1980, Carter continued to attack Reagan. Reagan had prepared for Carter to be aggressive and waited for his chance. When Carter said Reagan was a threat to world peace, Reagan deflected the criticism by smiling, shaking his head, and saying, "There you go again." The line drew a laugh from the audience. Carter further hurt himself when he reported he had asked his twelve-year-old daughter, Amy, what she thought was the most important issue of the campaign. Her reply was nuclear weapons and arms control. Reagan supporters regarded it as another effort to portray Reagan as a war-monger, while Carter supporters thought it made the president look like he was asking his daughter for campaign advice. Either way, it was a bad decision on Carter's part. The day after the debate, most polls declared Reagan the decisive winner of the debate, but did not detect a shift of voters to Reagan.

On the last weekend before the election, it looked like Iran might release the fifty-two hostages, which could have swung the election to Carter. Reagan avoided commenting on the possibility. He did not want to look like a political opportunist by taking advantage of a tenuous situation. "All I can tell you is I think this is too sensitive to make any comment on it at all," he said.

Unfortunately for the Carter campaign, the last minute negotiations were fruitless. In his final campaign speech, Reagan asked the voters a few simple questions. Were they financially better off than they were four years ago? Were they happier in 1980 than they were in 1976? Did they think America was stronger than it was four years earlier? If the answer was yes, they should vote for Carter. If not, then they should vote for a change.

As the campaign ended, all Reagan could do was wait for the public to respond with their votes. On Tuesday, November 4, 1980, Reagan received his answer. Before the polls on the West Coast had even closed, the television networks reported a landslide for Reagan. Two hours before the polls closed in California, Carter called Reagan and congratulated him on his victory.

Reagan received over eight million more votes than Carter. He won fifty-one percent of the popular vote, compared to forty-one percent for Carter, and seven percent for John Anderson, an independent candidate. Reagan won the electoral votes of forty-four states, which gave him a lopsided 489 to 49 margin over Carter in the Electoral College. Reagan's popularity also carried over into the congressional elections. The Republicans picked up twelve seats in the Senate, enough to win control for the first time in twenty-eight years. The Democrats were able to maintain control of the House, despite losing twenty-eight seats.

After the election, pollsters tried to explain how Reagan had won what was supposed to be a close election by such a large margin. Carter's low approval rating was one reason, they decided. Another was that Carter and the Democrats underestimated Reagan as a campaigner and candidate. Perhaps the most important reason was Reagan's ability to attract Democrats. He presented a platform of lower taxes, less government regulation, a stronger military, and patriotism and pride. The message appealed to independents and Democrats, as well as Republicans. His personable demeanor, polished over forty years in entertainment and politics, helped take the edge off of his hard-edged comments.

On November 20, 1980, Reagan met with Carter in the Oval Office for a private briefing. The outgoing president spent an hour updating the president-elect about the issues he would be facing. During the meeting, Reagan did not ask any questions or make any remarks. He took no notes. He asked Carter for copies of his notes for his staff. He would not read them himself. He planned for his aides to implement the major policy decisions. Carter had been criticized for being too involved in governmental affairs. Reagan was going to employ a much more hands-off leadership style.

Chapter Nine

President Reagan

Reagan's inauguration day, January 20, 1981, was a day of high drama. While he took the oath of office as the fortieth president, the fifty-two American hostages who had been held in Iran for 444 days were set free. The night before the ceremony, Jimmy Carter and his administrative staff firmed up the final negotiations for their release. The terms of release included the return of Iranian assets frozen by the Carter Administration and the freezing of the assets of the country's former ruler. The United States also promised not to interfere in the internal affairs of Iran and to remove the trade restrictions between the two countries.

At 11:57 A.M., as Reagan stepped to the podium to take the oath of office, sunlight broke through the cloudy sky. Standing in front of the Capitol overlooking the city, he placed his hand on a Bible held by Nancy and swore to fulfill his duties as president of the United States. In his inaugural address, Reagan repeated his pledges to curb the size and scope of the federal government and to mend the faltering economy.

> The economic ills we suffer have come upon us over several decades. They will not go away in days, weeks or months, but they will go away . . . In the present crisis, government is not the solution to our problems; government is the problem . . . it is my intention to curb the size and influence of the federal establishment . . . all of us need to be reminded that the federal government did not create the states; the states created the federal government.

Shortly after the ceremony, the new president announced the release of the American hostages. The Iranians had held up the plane carrying the hostages until Reagan took his presidential oath.

Upon entering the White House, Reagan's first item of business was to convince Congress to pass his economic policies. When Reagan entered office, unemployment was 7.5 percent and inflation soared to over thirteen percent. Reagan's solution to the economic troubles of the late 1970s was nicknamed "Reaganomics" by the press. The main components of his plan, officially called supply-side economics, was to stimulate the economy through reduced taxes and to slow government growth by reducing spending.

By February, Reagan presented his plan to a joint session of Congress. Many opposed the proposed cut in tax rates, as well as the elimination of several welfare

Ronald Reagan took the presidential oath of office on January 20, 1981, and promised to begin a new era in American politics. (*Courtesy of the Ronald Reagan Library.*)

programs and federal regulations. Although Reagan usually employed a hands-off management style, he personally worked hard to persuade Congress to pass his policies. During the first four months he was in office, the president met nearly seventy times with congressmen and senators to lobby for his budget and tax cuts, as well as increased military spending. Working with congressional leaders and using his considerable powers of persuasion, Reagan got Congress to pass the Economic Recovery Tax Act of 1981. He had engineered the largest federal tax reduction in history.

After the reduction in tax rates, which were never matched by sizable cuts in federal spending, the budget deficit exploded and the stock market slumped. This was followed by a recession that would last nearly two years. Thousands of companies went bankrupt and unemployment rose significantly. In December 1981, Reagan received forecasts of huge budget deficits for the next three years. In 1982, the unemployment rate climbed to 10.8, the highest since the Great Depression four decades earlier. Congress, in an attempt to slow the growth of the deficit, approved tax increases of almost ninety-one billion dollars. In just one year, the nation's largest tax cut was followed by its largest tax increase. The public's response to the recession did not bode well for Reagan's chances of being elected to a second term. In 1982, in the midterm congressional elections, Republicans lost twenty-six House seats.

Although Reagan called for a balanced budget amendment during his two terms as president, he never submitted a budget that was close to being balanced. Government spending continued to grow at a high rate. After two years of recession, though, inflation diminished and the economy began to create new jobs. In 1982, the stock market began a long period of growth, and for the first time in fifteen years, Americans enjoyed an economic recovery. As the economy rallied and expanded, the unemployment rate fell to 5.3 percent by the end of Reagan's presidency.

Barely two months into his first term, in the midst of lobbying for his economic reforms, Reagan faced the most serious crisis of his life. On March 30, 1981, he left the Hilton Hotel in Washington after making a speech. Waving to the crowds as he approached his limousine, he heard a cracking sound. Responding immediately, Secret Service agent Jerry Parr pushed Reagan into the back of the limousine. The president felt an excruciating pain in his upper back and thought he had a broken rib. Then the president began coughing up blood. When Parr saw the blood, he ordered the driver, who had been headed back to the White House, to go immediately to George Washington Hospital. Many credit Parr's quick thinking with saving Reagan's life.

Reagan's would-be assassin had fired off six rounds in two seconds. One of the bullets ricocheted off the limousine, entered Reagan's left side, and hit a rib before puncturing and collapsing a lung. The bullet stopped one inch from his heart.

Reagan walked into the hospital unaided, but he soon collapsed. He had lost about three pints of blood and was having trouble breathing. Even while going through this life-threatening crisis, he displayed a remarkable sense of humor. When one of the doctors said they were going to operate, Reagan said, "I hope you're a Republican." A medical staff member responded, "We're all Republicans today." After two hours of surgery, Reagan made a remarkably quick recovery. Twelve days after being shot, he was back at the White House.

The gunman, John Hinckley Jr., was a former college student and mentally-ill drifter who was obsessed with actress Jodie Foster. He repeatedly watched her film *Taxi Driver,* in which there is an assassination attempt on a politician's life. Hinckley apparently believed he could win Foster's heart by killing Reagan. Hinckley was charged with attempting to kill the president and multiple charges of assault and illegal possession and use of a firearm. In addition to Reagan, his shots hit three other people. He pleaded not guilty by reason of insanity. In a seven-week trial, a federal jury agreed, and he was confined to a mental institution.

Although the shooting was traumatic for the nation, the humor that Reagan displayed generated respect and sympathy among members of Congress and the public. This translated into support for his economic plan, which was passed later in the year.

While domestically Reagan was working to reduce taxes and the size of the federal government, he was also spending large amounts of money to expand the military. Reagan came into the office convinced the United States should be more aggressive in its relations

Days after being seriously wounded in an assassination attempt, President Reagan posed with Nancy for the cameras. (*Courtesy of the Ronald Reagan Library.*)

with the rest of the world, particularly with regards to Communist states. His foreign policy focused on the Soviet Union, Central America, and the Middle East.

Although Carter had been able to get Israel and Egypt to sign a peace accord, Reagan was faced with conflict in the Middle East early in his presidency. The country of Lebanon was in turmoil, where there was a brutal war raging between Christians and Muslims. Southern Lebanon was occupied by military installations of the Palestinian Liberation Organization (PLO) that was committed to destroying the state of Israel. The PLO bombed Israel, located to the south. In 1982, Israel retaliated by invading Lebanon.

In an attempt to bring order to a chaotic situation, the U.S., France, and Italy sent peacekeeping forces to Beirut, the capital of Lebanon. In April 1983, angered by the Western presence, a suicide squad attacked the U.S. Embassy, killing sixty-three people. The U.S. retaliated with bombs, which increased tensions even more. In October, terrorists drove trucks packed with explosives into the four-story U.S. military barracks at the Beirut airport. The bombing killed 241 marines.

The bombing in Beirut was a stinging military defeat and a political setback for American efforts in Lebanon. Four months after the attack, Reagan moved the remaining marines out of Lebanon after a critical report issued by the Department of Defense concluded there had been too many men in a single building, and the security measures had been inadequate. This ended the U.S. effort to mediate the conflict in Lebanon, and the war there continued. Eventually, a number of Americans were seized and held as hostages by Arab groups fighting against Israel.

Criticism for the collapse of the American presence in Lebanon was muted by the successful invasion of the Caribbean nation of Grenada. Grenada, governed by a Marxist prime minister, had been receiving aid from Cuba for several years, including the construction of a large airport. Reagan believed the large runway would allow the Soviet Union and Cuba to bring in soldiers and arms. Things came to a head in October 1983, almost at the same time the marines were killed in Lebanon, when a more militant faction of Grenada's ruling party murdered the prime minister and proclaimed itself the new government. Reagan said this change in government presented a threat to the one thousand Americans on the island, most of them students at a medical school. He ordered an invasion to take place two days after the marines died in Lebanon. The quick victory in Grenada helped to deflect attention from the terrorist attack in Lebanon, and reassured Americans their nation was still militarily strong.

Chapter Ten

Morning in America

In January 1984, with the country's economy on the rebound, Reagan formally announced he would seek re-election. He had no challengers in the Republican Party and was able to rest while the Democrats campaigned to choose a candidate to oppose him in the general election.

After a contentious primary season, Walter Mondale, who had served as President Carter's vice president, won the Democratic nomination. Mondale faced an uphill campaign. Some political analysts believe his campaign was doomed from the start. He decided to draw a clear distinction between himself and Reagan during his acceptance speech at the Democratic convention. "Let's tell the truth. Mr. Reagan will raise taxes and so will I. He won't tell you. I just did."

Mondale chose Representative Geraldine Ferraro of New York as his running mate. Ferraro was the first woman to run as vice president on a national party ticket. She soon came under attack, however, when questions were raised about some of her husband's real estate dealings.

Now campaigning for his second term as president, Reagan's age—seventy-three—was once again an issue. Prior to the election, the White House staff publicized Reagan's robust good health and vitality. The magazine *Muscle Training Illustrated* called Reagan "the best physically fit president of all time," and shortly after his seventy-third birthday, Reagan's physicians announced he was completely recovered from the 1981 assassination attempt. White House staffers also had a photo shoot showing Reagan "overpowering" bodybuilder Dan Lurie in an arm-wrestling match.

During a debate, Mondale pointed out that Reagan was the oldest president in America's history. Reagan deflected the age issue by jokingly saying: "I will not make age an issue of this campaign. I am not going to exploit for political purposes, my opponent's youth and inexperience." After Mondale laughed at the quip, Reagan's age was no longer an issue.

Mondale charged that Reagan's economic policies favored the rich and that his foreign policy increased tensions between the U.S. and the Soviet Union. One gaffe by Reagan gave credence to this charge. When testing a microphone before delivering his weekly radio address, he remarked: "My fellow Americans. I am pleased to tell you today that I've signed legislation that will outlaw Russia forever. We begin bombing in five minutes." The Soviets complained about Reagan's comment and public opinion polls showed an increase in the number of Americans that were concerned Reagan would get the country involved in a war.

Mondale, however, was never able to cut into Reagan's lead. On November 6, 1984, Reagan carried forty-nine of fifty states and received 525 electoral votes, the largest majority in history. Reagan also received fifty-nine percent of the popular vote, 16.8 million more than Mondale.

Reagan's victory did not seem to help other candidates in his party. Republicans lost one seat in the Senate, although they still maintained a majority, and failed to gain control of the House of Representatives. Reagan would still have to deal with a politically divided Congress.

Due to unusually cold temperatures, which reached two degrees below zero, Reagan's second inaugural ceremony was moved indoors and the parade was cancelled. In 1873, Ulysses S. Grant was the only other president to cancel his parade due to frigid weather.

Reagan began his second term as he had his first, by focusing on the economy. In May, he proposed overhauling the tax code, saying he would make it simpler and fairer. This time he faced many opponents who were in his own party. Over the years, the tax code had been filled with loopholes and deductions that tended to favor real estate developers and others who contributed to the party. It took a huge lobbying effort, several compromises, and working with Democrats, before the Tax Reform Act of 1986 was passed by Congress.

Also early into his second term as president, Reagan publicly sent a warning to terrorists. "When the rules of international behavior are violated, our policy will be one of swift and effective retribution." He would soon have to stand behind his words.

In June 1985, Shiite Muslims hijacked a jet airliner flying to Athens, Greece, from Rome, Italy. Over one hundred Americans were among the flight's 153 passengers. The terrorists diverted the flight to Beirut, Lebanon, executed an American serviceman, and demanded the release of Shiite prisoners held in Israeli jails.

Although Reagan had often proclaimed the United States would not negotiate with terrorists, in this instance he backed down. Following two-and-a-half weeks of negotiations, the final thirty-nine Americans being held hostage were freed. In return, Israel released the Shiite prisoners it had been holding. Despite this arrangement, Reagan continued to insist no deal had been made with the terrorists. This mode of thinking would eventually lead him into the worse scandal of his presidency.

When possible, Reagan attempted to retaliate against terrorism. In October 1985, members of the PLO hijacked the Italian cruise ship *Achille Lauro*, bound for Egypt. They murdered an elderly, wheelchair-bound, Jewish-American passenger. When Egyptian authorities promised the Palestinians safe passage out of the country, the hijackers surrendered the ship and boarded an Egyptian airliner. Once in the air, U.S. Navy F-14 fighter jets surrounded the plane and forced it to land in Sicily, where the local authorities arrested the hijackers.

Reagan charged that five countries—North Korea, Cuba, Nicaragua, Iran, and Libya—were responsible for most of the terrorist acts being committed at that time. He singled out Libya and its dictator, Muammar Qaddafi, as the worst of the five. In April 1986, an American serviceman was killed and sixty other Americans were injured when a bomb exploded at a discotheque in West Berlin that was popular with American military personnel stationed in Germany. After U.S. intelligence identified Libya as being responsible for the bombing, Reagan ordered F-111 fighter jets to bomb Qaddafi's home. The bombings outraged many nations, who condemned it as an act of U.S. terrorism.

Still, Reagan's military actions were popular with many, who saw them as a reaffirmation of America's military might. However, he was criticized for his policy in Central America. Reagan opposed any hint of Communism in the Western Hemisphere. The focus of most of his anti-Communist attention was on two countries, El Salvador and Nicaragua.

In El Salvador, leftists supported by Cuba were trying to overthrow the military-dominated government. The Reagan administration supported the government with military and financial aid. Both the leftist guerrillas and the government forces were guilty of atrocities. Under pressure from the U.S., elections were held and a new government was installed, but the civil war continued until guerrilla forces signed a peace treaty in 1992, after Reagan left office.

In contrast to the situation in El Salvador, the leftist Nicaraguan government was in power when Reagan assumed office in 1981. The ruling party was known as the Sandinistas, and their opponents were called *contrarevolucionarios* or contras. In 1981, Reagan's administration reported that Nicaragua was sending arms to the rebels in El Salvador, and the U.S. Congress cut off aid. The U.S. also began to secretly send arms to the contras. The contras were commanded by military officers who had been a part of the former dictatorship that had been overthrown by the Sandinistas. Again, there were an appalling number of atrocities committed by both sides.

The aid to the contras, although always controversial, continued until 1984, when it was reported that the U.S. Central Intelligence Agency (CIA) had directed the mining of harbors in Nicaragua. This discovery prompted Congress to pass the Boland Amendment, outlawing military aid to the contras. Reagan ordered his aides to work around the law by raising private contributions to send to the rebels.

It was Reagan's combined dealings with the contras, and his willingness to negotiate with terrorists in the Middle East, that led to the Iran-contra scandal. Since the early 1980s, various groups in the Middle East, many linked to Iran, had kidnapped Western hostages, including seven Americans. The hostages were used in an attempt to force the U.S. and European nations to make concessions. Reagan had seen what the Iranian hostage crisis had done to the Carter presidency. He also felt a moral obligation to bring the American hostages home.

Iran and Iraq had been fighting an expensive and destructive war since 1980. The U.S. remained officially neutral, but in reality the Reagan administration supported whichever country was losing. The goal was to drag out the war as a way to keep either of the countries from dominating the oil-rich region. The hope was that after a long war, the two countries, both potential enemies of the U.S., would collapse in a stalemate.

Reagan later said it was his National Security Advisor, Robert McFarlane, who convinced him the U.S. should establish ties with a group of Iranians who were disenchanted with Iran's religious government led by the Ayatollah Khomeini. Reagan thought that after the ayatollah, who was old and not well, died, the moderates might be more willing to work with the United States. He also hoped they would pressure Khomeini to order the release of the American hostages.

One part of the negotiations involved selling weapons to the Iranians. This scheme met strong opposition from Secretary of State George Shultz and Secretary of Defense Caspar Weinberger. They argued it would undermine diplomatic efforts for peace in the Middle East and amounted to making secret deals with terrorists. Despite his repeated pledges never to make deals or negotiate with terrorists, Reagan, anxious to free the hostages, agreed to open a dialogue.

Over a period of several months, McFarlane and his successor, John Poindexter, made five secret sales of weapons to Iran. They arranged for the CIA to purchase arms from the Department of Defense. Then international arms merchants bought the weapons from the CIA and resold them to the Iranians. In return, the Iranians promised to help bring about the release of the American hostages.

Reagan's advisors then arranged for the profits made from the sale of arms to be diverted to the contras in Nicaragua. Oliver North, a Marine lieutenant colonel who served as an aide to McFarlane and Poindexter, set up the diversion of money to the rebels. The diversion of money from Iran involved the use of secret bank accounts and the establishment of dummy corporations for money laundering.

The scheme began to unravel on October 5, 1986, when a cargo plane used to transport supplies to the contras was shot down in Nicaragua and the American pilot, Eugene Hasenfus, was captured. Despite official denials from administration officials, Hasenfus was soon linked by reporters to the secret operation to provide arms to the contras.

Reagan waited until mid-November 1986 before he made a public statement about the arms-for-hostages and secret aid to the contras operations. By then, the Republicans had lost control of the U.S. Senate after the midterm elections. The scandal continued to grow as the news media found and reported new revelations. As Congress geared up for a full-scale investigation, the

Iran-contra affair began to look like the Watergate scandal all over again.

In a nationally televised address, Reagan defended the arms-for-hostages deals. The speech he made contained several statements that were not true. The most glaring misstatement was Reagan's assertion that all the "defensive" weapons and surplus parts received by Iran "could easily fit into a single cargo plane."

The address created a firestorm. Suddenly, President Reagan looked his age. Instead of the supremely confident "Great Communicator" Americans had come to expect, he reacted defensively to the negative publicity and attempted to deflect blame onto the media for his predicament, but it did not work. A poll in the *Los Angeles Times* showed only fourteen percent of Americans believed he had given an accurate version of the events in his address.

In an effort to contain the damage, Reagan appointed a special commission headed by former Texas Senator John Tower to investigate the Iran-contra scandal. In February 1987, the commission issued a critical report. It denounced the Reagan administration for secretly conducting arms-for-hostages operations while publicly urging other nations not to deal with Iran. In regards to aid to the contras, the Tower Commission placed the blame on Reagan for not overseeing his White House staff.

A special joint Senate committee held televised hearings that also cast the administration in an unfavorable light. Its final report charged that Reagan was responsible for the "secrecy, deception and disdain for the law" that characterized the operation. It also cited the Reagan administration for lying to and misleading Congress, destroying official documents, and failing to notify Congress of secret U.S. military operations. The fallout from Iran-contra continued for months. Lawrence Walsh was appointed as independent counsel by Reagan. Walsh secured indictments against North and Poindexter for fraud, conspiracy, and theft of government funds. McFarlane pled guilty to charges of withholding information from Congress. Secretary of Defense Caspar Weinberger was charged with lying to Congress and investigators about his role in Iran-contra, but he was pardoned by Reagan's successor, George Bush, before his case went to trial. North's charges were dismissed on a technicality.

The Iran-contra scandal was a serious blow to his legacy, but Reagan was able to put it behind him and finish his presidency with a foreign policy success.

Chapter Eleven

Perestroika

During his first press conference after being inaugurated in 1981, when reporters asked him when he would contact the Soviets to arrange a summit meeting, Reagan replied that arms control was not going to be a high priority in his administration. The Soviets could not be trusted, he said. "They openly and publicly declared that the only morality they recognize is what will further their cause, meaning they reserve unto themselves the right to commit any crime, to lie, to cheat."

This attitude was part of a long pattern of not trusting the Soviet Union. Republican Richard Nixon had made arms control a high priority of his administration. One of the things he and Secretary of State Henry Kissinger were most proud of was their policy of *détente*, or engagement, with the Soviet Union and their opening of relations with the People's Republic of China.

Reagan changed that position. He had condemned the Nixon Administration for *détente* and had no plans to try to reach agreements with Communist nations. In 1983, he called the Soviet Union an "evil empire," and "the focus of evil in the modern world" in a speech before a conservative Christian group. He argued that because the Soviet Union was far ahead of the U.S. in the arms race, he sought to build up the American military and defense. Part of his defense program included a proposal to build the strategic defense initiative (SDI), a system to shield the U.S. from enemy missiles carrying nuclear warheads. It was soon nicknamed "Star Wars" because the missiles defending the U.S. from attack would be based in space. Many scientists expressed doubts about the program's effectiveness, or even the possibility of it being operational anytime in the near future. Reagan continued to insist it could be a genuine defense and deterrent from nuclear attack. It was suggested that Reagan proposed the SDI as a ploy to get the Soviets to reduce their arsenal of nuclear weapons, something he always denied. "I've had to tell the Soviet leaders a hundred times that the SDI was not a bargaining chip," he wrote. "I've told them I'd share it with others willing to give up their nuclear missiles."

When the SDI was proposed, both the U.S. and the Soviet Union were engaged in a massive arms buildup. The Soviet Union had intermediate-range missiles, which could strike targets up to 3,400 miles away, aimed at the major cities of Europe. The U.S. also had intermediate-range missiles in Europe, and in 1983, upgraded its nuclear armaments in Europe.

During the first years of the Reagan Administration, the Soviet Union began suffering through a leadership crisis. A series of leaders—Leonid Brezhnev, Uri Andropov, and Konstantin Chernenko—were old and ill and facing death. Brezhnev had been the leader for fifteen years when Reagan came into office, and he died soon afterward. Andropov, the former head of the KGB, the Soviet intelligence agency, suffered from chronic kidney disease for years and was ill during his short reign. Chernenko, the next leader, served slightly over a year and was near death during a great portion of that time. When Reagan was asked early in this first term why he had not met with a Soviet leader, he responded, "They keep dying on me."

With the death of Chernenko in 1985, a new generation of leaders began to emerge in the Soviet Union. Mikhail Gorbachev, much younger than his predecessors, was chosen to be general secretary, or head, of the Soviet Union, by the Politburo, the Communist Party's ruling board.

Gorbachev had waited for years to get a chance to reform the Soviet Union. He saw that the economic system was not working and that there should be a lessening of political control over the Soviet people. He viewed himself as a preserver of socialism. Gorbachev was not in favor of a market economy, but he wanted to make the Soviet Union more democratic. He had twin names for his new policies: *glasnost* (openness) and *perestroika* (restructuring). Gorbachev wanted to slow the arms race. A reduction in military spending would free up more resources to rebuild his country's economy.

Reagan and Gorbachev agreed to hold summit meetings to improve U.S.-Soviet relations and discuss arms control. The two leaders met first in Geneva, Switzerland, in November 1985, then in Reykjavik, Iceland, in October 1986. The talks stalled over two issues: the Soviet Union's unwillingness to allow on-site inspections to ensure compliance with arms control treaties, and the United States continued work on a missile defense system.

Reagan wanted to find a balance between pressuring Gorbachev enough to compromise and pressuring him so much that he would be removed from power by the hard-liners in the Politburo. He knew Gorbachev had enemies who wanted to stop his reform efforts.

This need for caution did not deter Reagan from visiting the Brandenburg Gate in West Berlin, Germany. The gate was part of the Berlin Wall, which divided West Berlin from Communist East Berlin. It had become a symbol of the divide between East and West. Two and a half decades earlier, President John F. Kennedy had stood at the same location and expressed sympathy for the plight of the citizens of Berlin by stating: "Ich bin ein Berliner! [I, too, am a Berliner.]" Kennedy's goal had been to assure the citizens of Berlin he stood with them in their resistance to Soviet control. In his address, Reagan threw down a challenge to the leader of the Soviet Union: "General Secretary Gorbachev, if you seek peace, if you seek prosperity for the Soviet Union and Eastern Europe, if you seek liberalization: Come here to this gate. Mr. Gorbachev, open this gate. Mr. Gorbachev, tear down this wall!"

Finally, Gorbachev agreed to allow mutual on-site inspections and to accept SDI. That led to the signing of the Intermediate-range Nuclear Forces (INF) treaty in December 1987, in which the world's two military superpowers agreed to totally eliminate intermediate-range missiles. This required the Soviets to destroy four times as many weapons as the United States. Both countries agreed to allow short-notice inspections on each other's soil until the end of the twentieth century. For the first time, two nations agreed to destroy, rather than build, nuclear missiles. Although the treaty reduced the actual number of nuclear weapons by just four percent, it held out hope for further reductions and signaled an improvement in relations between the two countries.

The lessening of tensions also benefited from the withdrawal of Soviet troops from Afghanistan in 1988. Nearly ten years earlier, the Soviets had invaded Afghanistan after a group of rebels known as the *mujahadeen* (holy warriors) tried to overthrow the country's Soviet backed government. President Carter had made several efforts to get the Soviets to withdraw. He stopped the sales of grain and high technology equipment and pressured the United Nations to pass a resolution condemning the invasion. When these steps failed, Carter pulled American athletes out of the 1980 Olympic Games in Moscow. Sixty-three other nations joined the U.S. in the Olympic boycott, but Soviet forces remained entrenched in Afghanistan.

In 1987, President Reagan delivered a speech before the Berlin Wall in which he challenged Soviet leader Mikhail Gorbachev to "tear down this wall." (*Courtesy of the Ronald Reagan Library.*)

During the Carter Administration, the *mujahadeen* received thirty million dollars in U.S. aid. In the Reagan years, the figure grew to six hundred million dollars. The funding increase enabled the CIA to set up camps in neighboring Pakistan to train Afghan rebels. Rebels learned how to blow up ammunition dumps, fuel depots, and bridges. The *mujahadeen* were also provided with rocket launchers and Stinger surface-to-air missiles for shooting down Soviet aircraft.

By the late 1980s, the Soviets were becoming weary of war. Like America had been in Vietnam, the military superpower was bogged down in a guerrilla war with no end in sight. In 1988, they began withdrawing troops. The withdrawal was completed in February 1989.

One unfortunate side effect of the U.S. support of the *mujahadeen* was the development of well-trained and well-armed radical Islamic fundamentalists who soon turned against the United States. After their success against the Soviet Union, which soon collapsed, many of the *mujahadeen* were convinced they had single-handedly destroyed a superpower.

Reagan continued to pressure Gorbachev to liberalize the Soviet Union. In May 1988, he spoke to students at Moscow State University and visited a monastery to call for religious freedom. On December 7, 1988, Gorbachev and Reagan met for the final time. The next day, Gorbachev addressed the United Nations and announced he would reduce the size of the Soviet military forces by half a million troops and withdraw a significant number of tanks and troops from the Soviet controlled nations of Eastern Europe.

In 1988, Soviet leader Mikhail Gorbachev and President Reagan signed a treaty that drastically cut each country's stockpiles of nuclear weapons. (*Courtesy of the Ronald Reagan Library.*)

A few months after Reagan left office, in November 1989, the Berlin Wall came tumbling down, and Communist East Germany and the democracy of West Germany were reunited as one nation. The people in the other Soviet satellite countries of Poland, Czechoslovakia, Hungary, Romania, Bulgaria, Albania, and Yugoslavia replaced their Communist governments as well. Unlike in the past, the Soviets did not send in troops to restore Communist control. Inside the Soviet Union, elections were held and many Communist Party members were replaced with politicians who wanted to try a market system. Former U.S. Secretary of State Henry Kissinger acknowledged that although George Bush was president when the Soviet Union collapsed, "it was Ronald Reagan's presidency which marked the turning point." Reagan's stance toward the Soviet Union was the culmination of the containment policy that had begun under President Truman's presidency in the late 1940s.

Another area where Reagan had an impact is the federal judiciary system. He appointed seventy-eight appeals court judges and 290 district court judges, over half of the members of the federal judiciary. He made three appointments to the nine-member U.S. Supreme Court. His first appointee, Sandra Day O'Conner, fulfilled a campaign pledge to appoint the first woman to the Supreme Court. His other appointees were Anthony Scalia in 1986 and Anthony Kennedy in 1988. He also selected a sitting Associate Justice, William Rehnquist, to be chief justice. These selections altered the court, which began to shift its focus from expanding constitutional protections to a more conservative position.

Although he was able to appoint many conservatives to the courts, Reagan was not able to get his way every time. In 1987, he nominated circuit court judge and former professor Robert Bork to the Supreme Court. After a bitter fight, in which many of Bork's writings sought to limit the reach of civil rights laws and that argued against a constitutionally protected right to privacy were made public, Bork was rejected by the Senate with a vote of fifty-eight to forty-two.

During Reagan's second term, the U.S. space program suffered its worst disaster in history. On January 28, 1986, the space shuttle *Challenger* took off from the Kennedy Space Center. Among its seven crew members was a civilian schoolteacher, Christa McAuliffe, who had been selected to be the first teacher in space. There were many spectators on the ground, as well as children watching on televisions in their classrooms. Seventy-three seconds into the flight, the shuttle exploded, killing all on board. A State of the Union speech was scheduled for that same day, and Reagan spoke of the tragedy. "The crew of the space shuttle *Challenger* honored us by the manner in which they lived their lives. We will never forget them, nor the last time we saw them, this morning, as they prepared for the journey and waved good-bye and slipped the surly bonds of earth to touch the face of God."

Although George Bush had been a loyal vice-president for eight years, Reagan did not rush to endorse him as his successor. One biographer of Nancy Reagan has claimed that Nancy did not want her husband to support Bush early in the 1988 presidential primary campaign. Bush had to fight off challenges from Kansas Senator Bob Dole and Christian television evangelist Pat Robertson to win the nomination. Finally, on May 11, 1988, after Bush was almost assured the nomination, Reagan endorsed his vice president at a Republican Party fund-raising dinner in Washington, D.C. Some party activists were puzzled by how brief and restrained Reagan was in his endorsement.

Once Bush became the Republican nominee, however, Reagan became a more enthusiastic supporter. He viewed the 1988 presidential election as a referendum on his policies and administration, and he made at least one campaign speech a week for Bush.

On November 8, 1988, the Republican ticket of Vice President George Bush and Indiana Senator Dan Quayle defeated their Democratic opponents, Massachusetts Governor Michael S. Dukakis and Texas Senator Lloyd Bentsen. On January 20, 1989, George Bush was inaugurated as America's forty-first president. In his inaugural address, Bush paid homage to his predecessor: "There is a man here who has earned a lasting place in our hearts and in our history. President Reagan, on behalf of our nation, I thank you for the wonderful things you have done for America."

Chapter Twelve

Last Years

When Reagan left the White House, he returned to California and moved to a home in Bel Aire. He went back to his old job, making speeches, and soon found himself criticized for collecting large fees for his personal appearances. He charged fifty thousand dollars a speech and collected over $750,000 in fees during his first three weeks as an ex-president. In the fall of 1989, he collected a two million dollar fee from the Fujisankei Communications Group in Tokyo for making two twenty-minute speeches and a few personal appearances during a ten-day visit to Japan. Reagan defended his actions by citing the salaries he received as governor and as president. "I just thought that in sixteen years I hadn't made any kind of money," he said.

The federal government provided him an office near Los Angeles, which he visited once or twice a week. Some of his time was spent on the creation of the Reagan Library in Simi Valley, California, outside of

Los Angeles, which was dedicated on November 4, 1991. Along with Reagan, Presidents Bush, Carter, Ford, and Nixon were in attendance. For the first time in history, five American presidents were together at the same time and place.

In the summer of 1992, the Iran-contra scandal was still being investigated, and Independent Counsel Lawrence Walsh wanted to question the former president. After several hours together, Walsh decided to forgo further interviews, as it was apparent that Reagan had experienced a great deal of memory loss. In November 1994, Reagan publicly confirmed he was suffering from the early stages of Alzheimer's disease, which causes increasing memory loss and impairs a person's ability to perform basic tasks.

In a public letter addressed to "My Fellow Americans," Reagan wrote: "At the moment I feel fine, I intend to live the remainder of the years God has given me on this earth doing the things I have always done. I will continue to share life's journey with my beloved Nancy and my family . . . I now begin the journey that will lead me into the sunset of my life. I know that for America there will always be a bright dawn ahead."

Reagan began to limit his public appearances and soon withdrew totally from public life. On February 11, 2002, he quietly observed his ninety-first birthday, becoming America's oldest living ex-president. In an interview with CNN's Wolf Blitzer, Reagan's son, Michael, described his father's life: "A typical day is—he sleeps very late. And sometimes I'm able to catch the moments

Former President Reagan and First Lady Nancy board the presidential helicopter one last time to begin the journey home to California on January 20, 1989. (*Courtesy of the Ronald Reagan Library.*)

when he is awake so I can visit . . . And every day the world gets a little smaller for him. It's just sad that he is not able to really understand how people feel about him and how much they love him."

How will Reagan be remembered? His presidency covered a period of dramatic change during which the Soviet Union began the process of unraveling. After the first two years of a severe recession, the U.S. entered a period of economic growth, low inflation, and high employment. He committed to spending large amounts of money on the military, which helped to force the Soviet Union into real disarmament negotiations.

On the negative side was the Iran-contra scandal, huge budget deficits, and decreased spending for programs to help the poor, the elderly, and the homeless. He did little to close the racial divisions that continue to plague American democracy, and shifted a higher portion of the tax burden from the wealthier people and businesses to middle class citizens.

There is little question that Reagan revitalized the Republican Party after the nadir caused by the Watergate scandal and the resignation of Richard Nixon. He also moved the conservative movement into predominant position within the party. In addition, he used his exceptional skills as a speaker to begin the process of restoring America's confidence that had been undercut by the Vietnam War and Watergate.

The most interesting aspect of Ronald Reagan, the man, is how much he remains a mystery. Journalist, Reagan biographer, and longtime acquaintance Lou

Cannon acknowledged: "I regard Reagan as a puzzle. I am still trying to understand the man." Many others remarked on this aloof quality that allowed thousands to admire him but few, if any, to ever feel that they truly knew or understood him.

Reagan was a man of contradictions. He spoke often of his Christian faith, but he seldom went to church. He advocated family values, and won much of his support from the conservative Christian movement, but he was a divorcee with a mostly distant relationship with his children and grandchildren.

In a way, Reagan remained an actor his entire life. Off the stage he was difficult to know or understand; on stage he could stir the emotions of thousands. Who he was as a man is difficult to grasp, but his impact on America will continue to be felt well into the twenty-first century.

Timeline

1911 Ronald Reagan is born, February 6.

1921 Reagan family moves to Dixon, Illinois.

1926-1933 Works as lifeguard on the Rock River.

1933 Becomes announcer for WHO in Des Moines, Iowa.

1937 Begins working in Hollywood for Warner Brothers.

1940 Marries Jane Wyman.

1941 Daughter Maureen is born.

1942 Drafted into the U.S. Army.

1945 Adopts son Michael.

1947 Elected president of the Screen Actors Guild.

1948 Divorces Jane Wyman.

1952 Marries Nancy Davis; birth of daughter Patricia Ann.

1954-1962 Works as host of *General Electric Theater*.

1958 Birth of son Ronald Prescott.

1967-1974 Serves as governor of California.

1981-1988 Serves as fortieth president of the United States.

1981 Shot by assassin, John Hinckley Jr.

1983 Bombing of U.S. embassy and military barracks in Beirut, Lebanon; invasion of Grenada.

1986 Space shuttle *Challenger* explodes.

1987 Report on Iran-contra scandal released; signing of Intermediate-range Nuclear Forces (INF) treaty with the Soviet Union.

1994 Diagnosed with Alzheimers.

Sources

CHAPTER ONE: "Drama, Politics and Sports"

p. 9, "If I had gotten . . ." Ronald Reagan, *An American Life* (New York: Simon and Schuster, 1990), 19.

p. 9, "all I got was rejection . . ." Ibid., 20.

p. 12, "I learned from my father . . ." Ibid., 22.

p. 13, "I loved three things . . ." Ronald Reagan and Richard G. Hubler, *Where's The Rest of Me?* (New York: Duell, Sloan and Pearce, 1965), 6.

p. 14, "Giving that speech . . ." Ibid., 48.

p. 15, "when the bottle . . ." Ibid., 53.

p. 16, "I'd been taught a lesson . . ." Ibid., 53.

p. 16, "(He) Just couldn't execute . . ." Anne Edwards, *Early Reagan: The Rise to Power* (New York: Morrow, 1987), 88.

p. 17, "and in about a quick hour . . ." Lou Cannon, *Reagan* (New York: G.P. Putnam's Sons, 1982), 39.

p. 17, "By my senior year . . ." Reagan, *An American Life*, 59.

p. 19, "How in the hell . . ." Cannon, *Reagan*, 44.

p. 20, "Could you tell me . . ." Ibid., 63.

p. 20, "Here we are in the fourth . . ." Reagan, *Where's The Rest of Me?*, 50.

p. 20, "We return you now . . ." Ibid.

CHAPTER TWO: Sportscaster to Movie Star

p. 22, "The secret of announcing . . ." Cannon, *Reagan*, 45.

p. 25, "Look, Joy told me . . ." Reagan, *Rest of Me*, 72.

p. 25, "Max is the only . . ." Ibid.

p. 26, "Max, I have another Robert Taylor . . ." Ibid.

p. 26, "I've got to get back . . ." Reagan, *An American Life*, 80.

p. 27, "SIGN BEFORE THEY CHANGE . . ." Ibid., 81.

p. 28, "*Love Is on the Air* presents . . ." Ibid., 86.

p. 29, "It was the springboard . . ." Tony Thomas, *The Films of Ronald Reagan* (Secaucus, N.J.: Citadel Press, 1980), 104.

CHAPTER THREE: Transitions

p. 33, "You really should give this . . ." Thomas, *Films of Reagan,* 142.

CHAPTER FOUR: Un-American Activities

p. 38, "I do not believe . . ." Edwards, *Early Reagan*, 348.

p. 38, "suspected of more or less . . ." Ibid., 344.

p. 39, "Probably because of my dad's influence . . ." Reagan, *An American Life*, 119.

p. 39, "Our federal bureaucracy expanded . . ." Ibid., 120.

p. 40, "I'm going to pick my own pictures . . ." Cannon, *Reagan*, 66.

p. 40, "I was footloose . . ." Ibid., 89.

p. 42, "I knew that being his wife . . ." Kitty Kelley, *Nancy Reagan: The Unauthorized Biography* (New York: Simon & Schuster, 1991), 72.

p. 43, "There's a wall . . ." Dinesh D'Souza, *Ronald Reagan: How an Ordinary Man Became an Extraordinary Leader* (New York: Touchstone Books, 1997), 7.

CHAPTER FIVE: Politics and Television

p. 46, "I literally traveled . . ." Edwards, *Early Reagan*, 73.

p. 46, "it would make my job easier" Cannon, *Reagan*, 96.
p. 48, "There's no way that I could . . ." Ibid., 96.
p. 48, "That's it . . ." Ibid., 96-97.
p. 50, "You and I have a rendezvous . . ." Reagan, *Rest of Me*, 312.
p. 52, "We checked with people . . ." Cannon, *Reagan*, 104.
p. 52, "We had reservations about Reagan . . ." Ibid.
p. 52, "an open and candid person . . ." Ibid.

CHAPTER SIX: Governor Reagan
p. 53, "As I have stated . . ." Lee Edwards, *Reagan: A Political Biography* (San Diego: Viewpoint Books, 1967), 104.
p. 54, "I thought it was a joke . . ." Kelley, *Nancy Reagan*, 139.
p. 54, "Reagan is only an actor . . ." Reagan, *An American Life*, 151.
p. 57, "a gimmick that solved nothing . . ." Cannon, *Reagan*, 122.
p. 57, "We are going to squeeze . . ." Ibid.
p. 58, "Over time, I gained . . ." Reagan, *An American Life*, 160.
p. 59, "My feeling was . . ." Cannon, *Reagan*, 159.
p. 60, "No one is compelled . . ." Edmund Morris, *Dutch: A Memoir of Ronald Reagan* (New York: Random House, 1999), 344.
p. 60, "Reagan has failed . . ." Paul O'Neil, 'The hottest candidate in either party," *Life*, October 30, 1970, 27.
p. 60, "a demagogue, a hypocrite . . ." Cannon, *Reagan*, 175.
p. 62, "I shared an image . . ." Ibid., 179
p. 62, "Look governor . . ." Ibid., 180.

CHAPTER SEVEN: Campaigning for President
p. 69. "Lay me down . . ." Cannon, *Reagan*, 226.

p. 73, "I would not go . . ." *Congressional Quarterly's Guide to U.S. Elections Third Edition.* Washington: Congressional Quarterly Inc., 1994, 142.

p. 73, "far different structure" Ibid.

p. 73, "I never envisioned . . ." Reagan, *An American Life,* 215.

p. 73, "Look, this isn't gonna work . . ." Ibid., 215

p. 75, "I tried to get to know Reagan . . ." Gerald R. Ford, *A Time to Heal: The Autobiography of Gerald R. Ford* (New York: Harper & Row and The Reader's Digest Assoc. Inc., 1979), 294.

p. 75, "George, it seems to me . . ." Reagan, *An American Life,* 216.

CHAPTER EIGHT: Second Try

p. 80, "There you go again . . ." William DeGregorio, *The Complete Book of U.S. Presidents* (New York: Barricade Book, 1993), 644.

p. 81, "All I can tell you . . ." Cannon, *Reagan,* 299.

CHAPTER NINE: President Reagan

p. 84, "The economic ills we suffer . . ." Reagan, *An American Life,* 226-227.

p. 88, "I hope you're a Republican . . ." Ibid., 261.

CHAPTER TEN: Morning in America

p. 92, "Let's tell the truth . . ." Lou Cannon, *President Reagan: The Role of a Lifetime* (New York: Simon & Schuster, 1991), 511.

p. 93, "best physically fit president . . ." *The New York Times,* January 9, 1984, Section III, 2.

p. 93, "I will not make age . . ." Cannon, *Role of a Lifetime,* 550.

p. 93, "My fellow Americans . . ." Frances Fitzgerald, *Way Out There in the Blue: Reagan, Star Wars and the End of*

the Cold War (New York: Viking, 2001), 240.
p. 95, "when the rules of international behavior . . ." Neal E. Robbins, *Ronald W. Reagan: 40th President of the United States* (Ada, Okla.: Garrett Educational Corporation, 1990), 99.
p. 100, "could easily fit . . ." Cannon, *Role of a Lifetime*, 683.
p. 101, "secrecy, deception and disdain for the law" Peter Kornbluh, "Iran-contra affair," *World Book Encyclopedia*, 2002, Vol. 10, 407.

CHAPTER ELEVEN: Perestroika
p. 102, "They openly and publicly declared . . ." D'Souza, *Extraordinary Leader*, 134.
p. 103, "the focus of evil . . ." Cannon, *Role of a Lifetime*, 316.
p. 103, "I've had to tell the Soviet leaders . . ." Reagan, *An American Life,* 548.
p. 109, "it was Ronald Reagan's presidency . . ." D'Souza, *Extraordinary Leader*, 196.
p. 112, "There is a man here . . ." Kelley, *Nancy Reagan*, 513.

CHAPTER TWELVE: Last Years
p. 113, "I just thought that in sixteen years . . ." Kelley, *Nancy Reagan*, 522.
p. 114, "At the moment I feel fine . . ." Morris, *Dutch*, 665-666.
p. 114, "A typical day is . . ." The Reagan Legacy. CNN Wolf Blitzer Reports. www.cnn.com/CNN/Programs/wolf.blitzer.reports/index/html.
p. 117, "I regard Reagan as a puzzle . . ." D'Souza, *Extraordinary Leader*, 7.

Bibliography

Brooks, Tim, and Earle Marsh. *The Complete Directory to Prime Time Network TV Shows 1946-Present.* New York: Ballantine Books, 1992.

Cannon, Lou. *President Reagan: The Role of a Lifetime.* New York: Simon & Schuster, 1991.

_____. *Reagan.* New York: G.P. Putnam's Sons, 1982.

Congressional Quarterly's Guide to U.S. Elections Third Edition. Washington: Congressional Quarterly Inc., 1994.

D'Souza, Dinesh. *Ronald Reagan: How an Ordinary Man Became an Extraordinary Leader.* New York: Touchstone Books, 1997.

DeGregorio, William A. *The Complete Book of U.S. Presidents.* New York: December Books, 1984.

Edwards, Anne. *Early Reagan: The Rise to Power.* New York: Morrow, 1987.

Edwards, Lee. *Reagan: A Political Biography.* San Diego: Viewpoint Books, 1967.

Evans, Rowland, and Robert Novak. *The Reagan Revolution.* New York: E.P. Dutton, 1981.

Fitzgerald, Frances. *Way Out There in the Blue: Reagan, Star Wars and the End of the Cold War.* New York: Viking, 2001.

Ford, Gerald R. *A Time to Heal: The Autobiography of Gerald R. Ford.* New York: Harper & Row and The Reader's Digest Association Inc., 1979.

Kelley, Kitty. *Nancy Reagan: The Unauthorized Biography.* New York: Simon & Schuster, 1991.

Kornbluh, Peter. "Iran-contra affair," *World Book Encyclopedia*, 2002, Vol. 10.

Leipold, L. Edmond, *Ronald Reagan: Governor and Statesman*. Minneapolis: T.S. Denison & Company, 1968.

Morris, Edmund. *Dutch: A Memoir of Ronald Reagan*. New York: Random House, 1999.

Moritz, Charles, ed. *Current Biography Yearbook 1967*. New York: H.W. Wilson, 1967.

Newcomb, Horace, ed. *Museum of Broadcast Communications Encyclopedia of Television. Vol. 3, Q-Z*. Chicago and London: Fitzroy Dearborn Publishers, 1997.

O'Neil, Paul. "The hottest candidate in either party." *Life*, October 30, 1970.

Reagan, Ronald. *An American Life*. New York: Simon and Schuster, 1990.

Reagan, Ronald, and Richard G. Hubler. *Where's the Rest of Me?* New York: Duell, Sloan and Pearce, 1965.

Robbins, Neal E., *Ronald Reagan: 40th President of the United States*. Ada, Okla.: Garrett Educational Corporation, 1990.

Rothe, Anna, ed. *Current Biography: Who's News and Why*. New York: H.W. Wilson, 1949.

Schlesinger, Arthur M. Jr., ed. *The Almanac of American History*. Greenwich, Conn.: Barnes & Noble Books, 1993.

Thomas, Tony. *The Films of Ronald Reagan*. Seacaucus, N.J.: Citadel Press, 1980.

Wiggins, D. Joel. "Ronald Reagan" *The Encyclopedia of Television, Vol. 3*. Chicago: Fitzroy Dearborn Publishers, 1997.

Websites

Ronald Reagan Library: www.reagan.utexas.edu

Ronald Reagan Foundation: www.reaganfoundation.org

Pictorial History and Selected Speeches of Ronald Reagan:
www.victorian.fortunecity.com/manet/404/index.htm

Ronald Reagan, The Official Site: www.ronaldreagan.com

Index

Slade Media Center